BEAR
An Autobiography

BEARDSLEY
An Autobiography

Peter Beardsley
with Andy Cairns

Stanley Paul
London   Sydney   Auckland   Johannesburg

Stanley Paul and Co. Ltd
An imprint of the Random Century Group
Random Century House, 20 Vauxhall Bridge Road, London SW1V 2SA

Random Century Australia (Pty) Ltd
20 Alfred Street, Milsons Point, Sydney, NSW 2061

Random Century New Zealand Limited
191 Archers Road, PO Box 40–086, Auckland 10

Century Hutchinson South Africa (Pty) Ltd
PO Box 337, Bergvlei 2012, South Africa

First published 1988
Revised edition 1990

Printed and bound in Great Britain
by Cox & Wyman, Reading, Berkshire

British Library Cataloguing in Publication Data
Beardsley Peter
  Beardsley: an autobiography
  1. Association football. Beardsley, Peter
  I. Title   II. Cairns, Andy
  796.334'0928

ISBN 0 09 174142 4

For Sandra and Drew

CONTENTS

1
CHAMPIONS

It was Ray Houghton who created the chance. His pass found me in space wide on the right on the edge of the Tottenham penalty area. The ball was easy to control and I moved forward towards the goal. Gary Mabbutt was the nearest defender but I knew that if I could quickly get inside the box he would have to be careful about any challenge. Gary tried to close down the space but as I cut back I could see a gap. I tried the shot. For a moment, I thought the Tottenham goalkeeper, Bobby Mimms, had saved it but then I heard the roar from the capacity Anfield crowd. I'd scored. It was the goal that was to clinch the championship for Liverpool in this, my first season for the club. It was one of the greatest moments of my career.

That game against Tottenham will always stick in my mind. We'd needed one point to make sure of the League championship. Although it wasn't our best performance of the season I scored the only goal of the game and we were the champions. The champagne came out and the dressing room was invaded by photographers and reporters from radio, television and newspapers. They all wanted a picture or an interview. It was bedlam.

The experts were saying we were the best club side since the Tottenham team that won the double 27 years earlier. We'd led the championship since October and never really looked like being caught. We'd played some sparkling football and won the League, the most important competition in British football, in style.

We'd played to packed crowds everywhere we went, and although we'd dominated the League to such an extent that there were no serious challengers after Christmas we tried to keep our football entertaining. It was a pleasure to play alongside such talented footballers. The Anfield fans had played their part in our success. The Kop, in particular, had been marvellous to me, even early in the season when the critics said I was struggling.

The celebrations were to continue long into the night on Merseyside. The club's ninth League title in 13 years. Just another trophy for many of the people at Anfield but a more significant moment for me. In nearly ten years as a professional footballer it was the first medal I'd ever won.

Nine months earlier I'd joined Liverpool from Newcastle for a fee approaching £2 million. It made me the most expensive footballer in Great Britain – a reputation I had to learn to live with. My first season with the club had exceeded all expectations. Not only had we won the League, but in a few weeks I would be playing in an FA Cup final for the first time. Although that was to end in bitter disappointment it couldn't take the gloss off a marvellous season in which I'd even captained my country!

So much had happened over the last year, and that evening after we won the League, my wife Sandra and I celebrated my first real footballing success at home on our own. I nipped out for a take-away supper of fish and chips and we sat and reflected on the ups and downs of a footballer's life.

At that moment I was at the peak of my career – an England international and League champion. Yet only five years earlier I was in despair after being rejected by Manchester United. A disappointing six month trial at Old Trafford had left my career at a low ebb and the idea of a League championship medal seemed nothing more than a pipedream.

I had a faltering start as a footballer anyway and almost didn't make it as a professional. I'd been turned down by Gillingham and Cambridge, and I was 18 years old and working in a factory before Carlisle took a gamble and signed me as a professional.

Joining Carlisle was to prove the wisest move of my life. But when I played my first game against Workington Reserves I never expected my career would turn out as it has. I never dreamed I would go to play in Canada in the North American Soccer League with its wacky characters and razzmatazz. Or that I would play for my childhood favourites Newcastle alongside one of my great heroes, Kevin Keegan.

CHAMPIONS

I never thought that I would play for my country and take part in the finals of a World Cup, or that I would join Liverpool, the greatest team in Europe, and play alongside some of the best footballers in the world.

It all seemed so improbable in those far off days as a small boy in Newcastle.

2
EARLY DAYS

I was born in Newcastle on 18 January 1961. Elvis Presley was at number one with 'Are You Lonesome Tonight?' while Tottenham were dominating everything in football that season, going on to complete the League and Cup double. Liverpool were still in the Second Division. They finished third and just missed out on promotion.

The Beardsleys lived in a fifth floor flat in Longbenton, on the north side of Newcastle. I grew up in a family that was sport mad. My dad, Sammy, a long distance lorry driver, used to box when he was in the army, and both my brothers, George and Ronnie, were football crazy. The men easily outnumbered the women in the family – my mum Catherine and my younger sister Sandra. We were, and still are, a very close family, and I had a happy childhood.

Even then my main love was football. In the early 1960s there was less traffic around and it was quite safe to play in the streets. I was out every day with a group of friends and a junior size football. One of our favourite games was what we called 'lamp-posting'. Each boy was given a lamp-post which was his goal. He had to defend that and at the same time try to score by hitting someone else's post. These games lasted long into the evening, by which time we would imagine we were playing under floodlights.

Another popular pitch was around the lock-up garages which belonged to the flats. The garage doors were the ideal shape and size for a goal, although the neighbours used to get annoyed at the constant thud and echo every time we scored.

I remember going to buy my first pair of football boots from Woolworths, who seemed to supply most of the boys in our part of town. There were three schools near us and we played each other at football regularly. Because all the boys lived on the same estate everyone knew people at the other schools and there was tremendous rivalry. One of the first games I can remember playing was against one of those other schools. One of the boys brought a small cup which was to be presented to the winners. We won the match, and although it was only a small, cheap, plastic trophy I felt as though I'd won the FA Cup.

My primary school, Somervyl, played in Burnley colours of claret and blue, although we later changed to canary yellow, similar to the Norwich City colours. I was one of the smallest in the class, and the games teacher, Mr Woodcock, used to play me on the right wing where he didn't think I would get hurt. Positions didn't mean much at that age though, and all 20 outfield players used to chase across the pitch in a pack following the ball.

When I was about ten the Beardsley family moved to a house in the Forest Hall district of Newcastle. The following year I changed schools, moving up to Longbenton High. I enjoyed my time there, although I wasn't the school's most outstanding academic success by a long way. I spent so much time playing football that I found it a real struggle to get down to doing any homework. In those days the highlight of the week would be Sunday afternoon. All the local boys used to wait for the men to come out of the pub on a Sunday lunchtime ready for a game of football in the local park. Quite often we would have 16 or 17 a side, and I would always try to be in the same team as my brothers.

It was around this time that I played my first serious game of football, where we were provided with a referee and a linesman. Wallsend Boys Club asked me to play against East End Boys Club. Peter Kirkley, a football fanatic, was in charge at Wallsend. He lived and breathed football, and later went on to become the youth development officer at Newcastle United.

That first game was one-sided to say the least. We won 17–2. It was so easy that at half-time we swapped our team around, pushing the defenders into attack and playing the forwards in defence. But even though we'd won I hadn't enjoyed the game. I preferred the idea of close contests with more evenly matched sides. At that time Wallsend Boys Club took the best boys from throughout the area. Consequently no other team could match them and they won easily every week. They asked me to join them permanently but I wasn't interested. I wanted to play in games which were more competitive, even if it meant a lower standard.

But by now I'd really caught the football bug. My parents bought me a pair of boots – Puma Pele Rio – which was the best present I think I've ever had. They were so comfortable that I used to wear them around the house. I always seemed to be dressed in football kit. One year my brother Ronnie bought me a replica of the new Coventry City strip for Christmas. It was at the time Coventry had introduced a new style and I thought this was fantastic. I wore the kit every day for months. It had to be washed at night so it would be dry, ironed and ready to wear again the next morning. I wouldn't be a day without it.

Like most of the boys from my area I was a Newcastle United fan. The first time I saw them play was in an evening match at St James's Park against Doncaster in the League Cup, as it was called then. We won 6–0, and I seem to remember that Frank Clark scored his first goal for Newcastle that night. I was only about nine years old, and I remember travelling to the match by bus with my brother George and his girlfriend. In those days it was quite common for Newcastle to attract crowds of more than 50,000. I'd never seen so many people and had never imagined that the ground would be so big.

We stood in the old Leazes End, and because I was so small I had to watch most of the game while perched on George's shoulders. It was the first time I'd ever been in such a big crowd and I was quite apprehensive. But the atmosphere was tremendous, the noise was deafening and the whole experience was more exciting than I had dreamed possible.

The player I admired more than any other was Jimmy Smith. He probably wasn't the best all-round footballer but was one of the most skilful. He used to try all kinds of tricks and delighted in 'nutmegging' – pushing the ball between his opponent's legs. He was a real character, exactly the kind of player the game needs.

The Newcastle team at that time also included Willie McFaul. He was in goal and later he was to be my manager at St James's Park. Bob Moncur, who was to become my manager at Carlisle, was in the back four with David Craig, Ollie Burton and Frank Clark. Tommy Gibb, Jimmy Smith and Tony Green were in

6

midfield with Malcolm Macdonald, John Tudor, Jimmy Sinclair and Pop Robson vying for position in attack.

My brothers, Ronnie and George, were Newcastle fanatics. They went to all the home games and travelled all over the country during the FA Cup run on the way to Wembley in 1974. I remember queueing all night for a ticket for the sixth round match against Nottingham Forest that season. I spent 12 or 13 uncomfortable hours in a sleeping bag on the pavement camped outside St James's Park with my brother Ronnie. In the morning my dad came round with some hot drinks to refresh us. There was tremendous excitement throughout the town that season and everyone in the queue was convinced that if we beat Forest we would be on our way to Wembley.

Unfortunately I never got to see the game, despite having queued for so long. I got my ticket without any problem but Ronnie decided that I was too young and too small to go to the game so he sold it to one of his mates. I was devastated at the time but in the end it worked out for the best.

The match was marred by a pitch invasion. Newcastle were losing 3–1 and were down to ten men when thousands of fans ran onto the pitch. There was pandemonium and the game was held up for eight minutes while the officials tried to restore order. My ticket had been for the same area where the trouble had started and, as I was only a little fellow, I would probably have been crushed in the crowd.

Newcastle went on to win that game 4–3, scoring three goals after the re-start. But the FA ordered an inquiry and decided that the invasion had changed the course of the game. They ordered a replay on a neutral ground, and United eventually went through after a second replay, Malcolm Macdonald scoring the only goal.

George and Ronnie went to the semi-final against Burnley at Hillsborough which we won 2–0 but once again I missed out. They both went to Wembley for the final but I was left at home and watched the match on television with my dad. I was dressed for the occasion in my Newcastle shirt, black and white scarf and hat, but the day ended in disappointment when we lost 3–0 to Liverpool. Kevin Keegan was magnificent in that game. He scored twice and continually tormented the Newcastle defence. I was 13 years old at the time and never dared to dream that one day I would go on to play in the same team as him.

By now I was playing football three or four times over a weekend and was training or playing games for the school or a youth club most evenings. My dad encouraged me. He thought that if I was playing football then I wouldn't be hanging around the streets and getting into trouble. In the summer we used to play cricket. I was a useful wicketkeeper but a hopeless batsman and always went in at number 11. But as much as I enjoyed summer sports I couldn't wait for the football season to come round again.

My main problem was my height, or rather lack of it. I was much smaller than other boys of my age and I didn't really start to grow until I was about 16 – and even that spurt was pretty short lived. But because I was so small I was always put out on the right wing where the games teachers and youth club organisers thought I wouldn't get hurt.

There were few signs that I would go on to make a career as a footballer. Some weeks I was left out of the school side, and although I went every year for trials with the county, South Northumberland, I was never picked for the team. The closest I got was being chosen as a substitute – the duties included running down to the chip shop to buy the pies for the rest of the team after the game.

I was given some encouragement by the games teacher at Longbenton, Mr Jimmy Giles. He was convinced that I was good enough and kept his faith in my ability. 'Don't worry son,' he used to say after I'd been overlooked once again. 'Your day will come!' To be honest there were some far better players around than me. Quite a few lads were invited to go training with Newcastle. Some were signed as apprentices, while a few made it all the way and became successful professionals. Steve Bruce, who used to play against us for Newcastle Boys, went on to play for Gillingham, Norwich and Manchester United; and Rob Hindmarch, who was the South Northumberland captain, went on to play for Sunderland and Derby.

I was quite happy playing for fun anyway. A few of my friends organised a team, and although we weren't that good I enjoyed playing for them as much as any other team I've turned out for. We were all mates and there's something special about being in a team with people who are friends. We'd all squash into the back of someone's car for trips to away games, and often we'd arrive at grounds where there were no changing rooms or showers, so we'd return home still covered in mud.

The North-East is football crazy. At weekends it seems as though every available patch of grass is turned into a football pitch. In those days as soon as one game finished there were 22 lads waiting to get on the pitch to start the next match.

Before long I was playing for my first men's team, my brothers' pub side – The Fusilier. The pub is only 200 yards from where we lived and my dad still goes there for his Sunday lunchtime pint. I was 16, and once again I was pushed out onto the right wing because I was so small. Inevitably I found it tough at times and I used to get the occasional kick from opponents who were bigger, older and more experienced than I was.

My brothers were prepared to let me grow up the hard way. They took no notice when I was on the receiving end of some rough stuff, and it was up to some of the other lads to come to my defence when the fists and boots really started to fly.

We had a successful team and it was quite a family affair for the Beardsleys. Brother Ronnie played at centre-half and was the team captain, while my brother George, who was much bigger than I was, played at centre-forward and was one of the best in the league. I was on the wing, whenever I could get a game, and my dad used to come along each week to cheer us on from the line. We enjoyed our share of success, reaching two cup finals and winning promotion in the same season.

My life revolved around football, and at weekends I did nothing else. I played for the school on Saturday mornings, the youth club in the afternoon, The Fusilier on Sunday mornings and Wallsend Boys Club on Sunday afternoons. I'd rejoined Wallsend following another invitation from Peter Kirkley. What persuaded me was the fact that they came to collect the players before a game and dropped them off at home afterwards. I was used to making my own way to games and hanging around in the rain waiting ages for a bus to come. Wallsend was luxury in comparison. The club was also very serious about its football. They weren't happy about me playing for The Fusilier a couple of hours before I turned out for them, but I loved playing for the pub side so much that there was no way I would give it up.

Around this time I contracted a gum disease and lost most of my teeth. I remember my dad taking me to the dentist to have 22 out in one go. I came out of the surgery with a huge scarf round my head, and for the next few days my mum spoiled me. She offered me loads and loads of ice-cream, but for the first time in my life I didn't feel like eating!

I left school at 16 with no prospect of a job, and, although I enjoyed my football, there seemed to be even less chance of a career as a professional. With unemployment so high in Newcastle I joined thousands of other school-leavers on the dole. I spent three months looking for a job before I got a chance to do a 12-week training course for basic engineering. Everyone who completed the course was supposed to be guaranteed a job. But once the 12 weeks were up there was no job and I had to go back on the dole.

We made the most of our time. I was a big Rod Stewart fan, and while my brother was at work I'd play all his LPs. I knew all the words to the early albums from 'Gasoline Alley' and 'Every Picture Tells A Story' through to 'Footloose and Fancy Free', which included the big hit of the day, 'You're in my Heart'.

Our main treat was a round of golf every Thursday. The giro arrived in the morning and I'd go off with a few friends to the local golf course for the rest of the day. My brother worked as one of the green-keepers, so we had no trouble getting a game.

There were so many people unemployed in the North-East that it was nothing unusual. But I wouldn't say it was enjoyable, and when one of my dad's friends offered me a job, labouring at the factory where he worked, I jumped at the chance.

It was tremendous to get up early every morning and walk to work with my brother George, who had a job as a fitter in another factory on the same industrial estate in Killingworth.

I worked for Young and Cunningham who made valves for ships. My responsibilities included sweeping the floors, cleaning the machines and running errands such as fetching lunches from the chip shop. Occasionally I got the chance to paint the valves. I earned between £25 and £30 a week. It seemed a marvellous wage.

I was still playing football for Wallsend Boys Club and still harbouring the dream of one day becoming a professional, although that seemed further away than ever. I was 17 and most lads who were going to make the grade had been with clubs since they were schoolboys. By my age they had completed their apprenticeships and were ready to sign on as full professionals.

But Peter Kirkley, who ran the Wallsend team, still thought I had the ability to make it, and he arranged for me to spend a week on trial with Gillingham. It was the other end of the country but I set off full of hope. Steve Bruce, another Newcastle lad, had already signed for Gillingham and I hoped to follow in his footsteps. I spent a week in digs and trained with the first team every day. I played in one friendly at the Priestfield Stadium but it wasn't a good game, and at the end of the week the manager, Gerry Summers, took me to one side and said: 'Thanks for coming but I'm sorry, I don't think you've got what it takes to be a professional.' It's a long way from Gillingham to Newcastle and I had plenty of time on the train journey home to reflect on what Gerry Summers had said. It hadn't been a good week, but despite Mr Summers' opinion it hadn't been bad enough to make me abandon my hopes of becoming a professional.

Peter Kirkley told me not to worry, and three months later he fixed me up with another week long trial, this time at Cambridge. That didn't work out either and I didn't even last the full week. I played in a friendly at Cambridge's Abbey Stadium against Newmarket and thought I had done quite well. But on the fourth day of the trial the Cambridge manager, John Docherty, took me to one side and told me he didn't think I was good enough to make it. One of the Cambridge coaches was going to Doncaster the next day and Mr Docherty had arranged for him to drop me at the station to get the train home to Newcastle.

Obviously I was disappointed. I went back to Newcastle and back to my job sweeping the floors in the factory. My dad kept me going. He knew I wanted to be a footballer and was convinced that I'd get my chance eventually. Everyone rallied round, and Peter Kirkley arranged for me to have further trials with Burnley, Carlise and Newcastle.

The boss at the factory wasn't too pleased to see me taking off even more time on what seemed to be a pointless pursuit of a career which never looked like getting off the ground. The company had been good to me, giving me a job when nobody else would. There were moments when I thought it would be wrong to take another day off and I was on the verge of not going to a couple of trials. But when I weighed up everything in my mind, the dream of becoming a footballer meant more than the reality of my steady factory job. I was getting on towards 19 and the chances being offered now would probably be my last.

For a Newcastle fan, the chance of a trial at the club I'd supported as a boy was too great an opportunity to miss. The club asked me to spend a week there. The first team were away on a pre-season tour of the West Country which meant I didn't see any of the big stars of the time, but I was happy enough walking around the ground where my heroes played. I was picked to play in a friendly against Marine Park, whose ground was near our home in Forest Hall. At the end of the game the reserve manager, Jimmy Nelson, came up and gave me £2 for my expenses. That was my first football wage. I felt great. I'd worn the Newcastle shirt for the first time and had been paid for it!

Most of the lads in our team were either apprentices or had been on trial like me. I hadn't scored but I felt I had done quite well, and as I was about to set off home Jimmy Nelson gave me some encouragement. 'Stick at it son,' he said, 'and there's a good chance you'll come to Newcastle.'

At last things looked as though they were moving. I'd had one game with Burnley and they seemed interested and were offering me a further two weeks trial. Things were going well with Newcastle when Carlisle phoned asking me to go along for a game one night that week. I'd already played in one trial match for their reserves at Brunton Park and had liked the set-up there. I had two days of my week with Newcastle to go, and although the club were indicating that they would like to sign me I felt the opportunity with Carlisle was too good to miss. It was one of the few times that I've ever told a fib when I phoned Newcastle to say I was ill and wouldn't be able to make it that day.

Much as I would have liked to play for Newcastle the club was not renowned for producing its own players at that time. They seemed to prefer splashing out in the transfer market rather than giving their youngsters a chance. Carlisle didn't have the money, or the vast number of players there were at Newcastle, and it seemed that with them I would have a greater chance of making the first team.

I'd been nervous at all my previous trials. At Gillingham and Cambridge I had felt as though I was an outsider. The other lads all knew each other. I was shy and only there for a few days so I didn't really get to know anyone. When I went into the changing rooms I was too scared to talk to anyone. The other lads were all laughing and there were plenty of in-jokes which, as an outsider, I obviously didn't understand. Once training was over everyone else went off and I was left on my own in a strange town.

They hadn't been happy times but now I was older and more experienced and boosted by the fact that a couple of other lads from Wallsend were going for a trial at Carlisle at the same time. It makes a tremendous difference when you play with people you know. At Gillingham and Cambridge I didn't know anybody's name to begin with and was very self-conscious during training.

I was also pleased that Carlisle had asked me to come back. Brian Watson was Carlisle's chief scout at that time and was instrumental in taking me there. Later Brian moved to Newcastle and I'm sure he was influential in persuading Arthur Cox to sign me from Vancouver, but unfortunately Brian had died before I came home. Ironically, his job as youth development officer at Newcastle was taken by Peter Kirkley who was also important in guiding me into a career as a professional. Back in 1979 both men were keen for me to join Carlisle. Having known nothing but rejections it was suddenly nice to feel wanted. So instead of training with Newcastle I dashed over to Brunton Park.

It was a marvellous night. I played well and scored the winning goal in a 3–2 win over Blue Star. Bobby Moncur, the Carlisle manager, also played that night and after the game he took me aside. I thought he was going to ask me for another trial game but when he spoke he nearly took my breath away.

'We'd like you to sign as a professional,' he said. I could hardly believe my ears. After so many disappointments, my dream had finally come true.

3
CARLISLE

I handed in my notice at the factory the following day. The boss thought I was making a terrible mistake and tried to talk me out of it, but, undeterred, I went to watch the Carlisle first team play a friendly in Darlington that night and signed a two-year contract as a professional after the game.

I was forced to work a week's notice at the factory so when I eventually joined Carlisle the players were well into their pre-season training. I'd missed the hardest parts but in my first week I was still expected to go on several five mile runs.

The other lads were used to it. I thought I was pretty fit but I'd never trained for more than a couple of hours on the odd evening after work. Suddenly I was doing more exhausting work and over longer and more regular periods. I'd never been strong on stamina but somehow I survived the runs and there were even one or two who lagged behind me.

Apart from my trials with Cambridge and Gillingham I'd never lived away from home before. Bobby Moncur, the Carlisle manager, must have known I was worried, and for the first five or six weeks he invited me and Stan Gates, who'd signed as an apprentice, to stay at his home. We were treated as part of the family and it helped me settle into my new surroundings. It was only 55 miles to Newcastle and Bobby allowed me to go home for weekends after the match on Saturday afternoon.

My first game for the club was away to Workington Reserves. We won 2–0. Graham Winstanley, who for some reason was known as a 'tot', scored the first and I added a second just before

14

half-time. I was delighted. It was my first goal for the club but it went largely unacknowledged by the rest of the team.

We went in at half-time feeling quite pleased with ourselves, but Bobby Moncur was furious. He felt the lads should have celebrated my goal with more enthusiasm. 'The lad is playing his first game, he does well to score a good goal and you lot ignore him,' he said. I felt quite embarrassed but I was pleased that the boss had noted my contribution.

I played for the reserves again the following Saturday. We beat Wrexham 5-2 in the Lancashire League and I managed to score a hat-trick. I'd been given the rest of the weekend off and went home to Newcastle feeling quite happy with my first week's work as a professional footballer. I thought I was settling in well and was doing enough to keep my place in the reserve team.

I went to watch my brothers play for The Fusilier on the Sunday morning and when we arrived home there was a telegram from Carlisle. They wanted me to return that evening and report for training the following morning.

I wondered whether I'd done anything wrong but once training was over the manager had a quiet word with me. 'How do you feel about playing for the first team tomorrow night?' he said. I couldn't believe it. I'd only been at the club a few days. A week or so earlier I'd been sweeping the factory floor and now I was set to play in the Football League.

The team had lost their opening match away against Southend. I was named in the side for the first home match of the season against Blackburn Rovers. It was 21 August 1979 and a crowd of 5801 turned up at Brunton Park to see us draw 1-1. I'm normally quite relaxed before a game and able to enjoy a laugh and joke in the dressing room, but that evening, for the first time in my life, I was terrified. I sat in the corner shaking. The evening paper had carried a big story about my first appearance, and although I was looking forward to playing I was worried about making a mistake and letting everyone down.

It was the first time that I'd played in front of a proper crowd and, although there were less than 6000 people there, they made a tremendous noise. Once the game got going my nerves disappeared and I wanted it to go on all night. Blackburn were one of the best sides in the Third Division. They were managed by Howard Kendall. He played that night and their team also included Duncan McKenzie. Paul Bannon scored our goal and in the end a draw was a fair result. Obviously I was tired and, even though I'd expected to be substituted, Bobby Moncur left me on for the whole game.

I'd played quite well and kept my place in the team for the game against Bury the following Saturday. We beat them 1–0 with a goal by Paul Bannon. But the following week I was left out for the trip to Millwall.

At the time their crowd was notorious for giving stick to the opposition. Bobby Moncur said he thought it best for me to be left behind. 'I think it's a bit too soon for you to play there,' he said. 'But don't worry, you'll be back in the team before long.' We lost 2–1 and I was back the following week.

At times I found it hard to adjust to life as a professional footballer. The team was expected to wear a suit and tie on match days. I'd never owned a suit and, more embarrassingly, I had to ask Jimmy Hamilton, one of the other lads, to show me how to put on a tie. I'd never worn one before.

I had trouble adjusting to things on the pitch as well. The game was much faster than anything I'd been used to. Players were fitter and also much quicker over the first couple of yards. Playing with professionals it was inevitable that my weaknesses would be exposed, in particular my heading, which was terrible. I also realised that I had a lot to learn about the game, and it took me a while to start thinking about how I could help our defence. Although I played up front I put our midfield and defence under pressure by allowing opposition defenders to go forward un-marked. It was only later that I fully realised how important it is for forwards to be aware of opponents running from deep to support their attack.

Initially I'd be left standing, hand on hips, while the opposition full-back rushed past me. I was always too slow to react but gradually Carlisle taught me to think one step ahead of my opponents. Martin Harvey, who was the coach, taught me to watch for the run from the back. He showed me that once the defender sees that you've got his run covered then he won't bother to go forward and you've restricted his team's options.

I started to get stronger, and as the season progressed the emphasis in training moved away from running and more towards ball-work. There was plenty of shooting practice and most days we'd have a five-a-side match. Some of the lads used to moan about training, but having been on the dole I probably appreciated the opportunity to play football for a living more than those who'd been doing it since they were apprentices. It was hard work at times but I certainly wasn't going to complain.

There were some great character at the club. Phil Bonnyman, Steve Hoolickin and Bobby Parker were always laughing and teasing the younger players. And they did their best to liven up the long journeys to away games. With Carlisle being the northernmost club in the Third Division by some distance we seemed to face an incredible journey every other week when we played away. I'd never been as far as places such as Exeter, Swindon and Plymouth before.

If we played an evening game the club would try to make the trip there and back in the same day to save the cost of a night in a hotel. Our coach would leave Carlisle around mid-morning, we would play the game, rush to get bathed and changed before leaving at half past nine and would arrive back in Carlisle in the early hours of the morning feeling absolutely shattered.

Sometimes we would stop for a steak after the game but more often than not the lads would want to get straight back home so we'd grab some fish and chips to eat on the coach. Every away trip was an adventure to me. I'd read about these grounds in the newspapers and was familiar with the teams from studying the football results, but I'd never been to any of these far-off places before. I was impressed when we played Portsmouth at Fratton Park. It looked like a First Division ground, and even though they were in the Third Division the team still drew crowds of around 14,000.

I also remember playing at Wimbledon in front of a crowd of 2093. We drew 0–0 and there was no hint at that time that Wimbledon would go on to become a First Division club. A few seasons earlier they'd been in the Southern League and their ground was so compact that the 2000 crowd were still able to create quite an atmosphere.

We did that trip, 650 miles there and back, in one day, stopping in London just long enough to play the game. The long journeys to away games meant we often met delays on the roads and arrived at the ground only a short time before kick-off. Some players were visibly upset by this as they were used to having an hour or so to prepare for a game, but it didn't bother me. I was used to arriving at grounds shortly before the kick-off with just enough time to get changed and onto the pitch before the captains tossed up. And many's the time I've had to get changed in the back of a van on the way to a game because we were running late.

In fact I found it unusual to have a full hour to get ready for a match. It only took me five minutes to get changed and tie my boots. I'd then have to sit around for 55 minutes waiting for the kick-off. I used to think: 'Well, what do I do now?' I was still very green and sat in amazement while other players went through their stretching exercises and warm-up routines. I thought only old players did stretches before a game and I'd never really done any before I joined Carlisle.

Home matches were the worst. We had to be at the ground by two o'clock so I *always* had an hour to kill before the game. Since then I've developed a routine where I get changed gradually and now I don't put my shirt on until moments before we go out on the pitch.

Some of the lads would warm up in the gym next to our changing room. But in my second season at Brunton Park the club built a new indoor training area with a plastic pitch. That wasn't quite as convenient for warming up. It was about 150 yards from the changing rooms and whoever designed it hadn't realised that the journey took us past the away fans. If it had been raining they took great pleasure in kicking water over us from the puddles on the path, and in deepest winter we'd have to run through a barrage of snowballs.

Carlisle were a friendly club. There was always a good atmosphere at Brunton Park, and the team regularly took a couple of hundred supporters to away games. Those fans were incredible. The players had it easy. All our travel arrangements were taken care of but the fans had to make their own way to the games, often at the other end of the country. Yet week after week we'd spot the same faces in the crowd and we appreciated what they were trying to do for us.

In my first six or seven games for Carlisle I played up front, but then Bobby Moncur moved me back into the right side of midfield. The game is always fast around that area and it sharpened my reactions, making me think and see things quicker.

I was lucky to have someone like Bobby Moncur as my first

manager. He said he'd signed me because I could dribble and he encouraged me to take on players, beat defenders and open up the game. At first I was worried about giving the ball away but Bobby insisted that I should try to play the way I had for my Sunday team. I'm lucky that whenever I do lose the ball it's always in the opponent's half of the field. They've got to go at least 50 yards to score so it's not often that I can give a goal away.

Bobby Moncur had a great influence on my career. I used to watch him when he played for Newcastle. He was an inspirational figure there and I never thought that he would one day guide me through my first days as a professional footballer. I initially signed for Carlisle on a two-year contract but after a couple of weeks, Bobby ripped that up and offered me a new four-year deal. Having spent some time on the dole, there was no way I was going to turn down security like that so I signed immediately. Bobby had only recently finished playing so he understood the way his own players thought and what they wanted. Without doubt Bobby Moncur had been one of the main reasons I'd joined Carlisle and I began to look forward to a long association with him.

Then I went in for training one morning to learn that Bobby had left to take over as manager at Hearts. I was shocked by the news. All my old doubts came back. Just when it looked like I had a career in front of me, the man who had offered me that opportunity had left.

It's always an unsettling time at a club when a manager goes. Players wonder what the new manager will think of them and who he'll want to get rid of. I was no exception, so it was a great relief when we were told that Martin Harvey, who'd been Bobby's coach, was to take over.

Martin was popular with the players and had worked hard to improve my game during training. That season, my first as a professional, Carlisle finished in sixth place in the Third Division. I'd played 37 League games and scored nine goals, including one in the FA Cup. It had been exhausting. I was still very small and had never known anything as tiring as the physical demands on a professional footballer. I think it was only the adrenalin that saw me through the season. Every game was such an adventure that I think I overcame the tiredness through sheer excitement. And everything was happening so quickly that I hadn't had time to stop.

But although the game was more physical than I'd been used to I'd escaped without getting too much of a kicking. I was lucky to have a big man like Paul Bannon playing up front who took most of the knocks. The big, hard defenders normally marked him and I was given a bit more freedom. But I was on the receiving end of one or two fierce tackles that season. The worst was the first. Ironically it was the work of Steve Bruce, who I knew from our days in schoolboy football in Newcastle, and who was by now playing for Gillingham. He caught me with a high tackle and with such force that for one moment as I lay on the ground in agony I thought I would never walk again. The memory of that incident still makes me wince.

But I'd enjoyed my first year and couldn't wait for the next season to arrive. Unfortunately we had a terrible start, and after losing 4–1 at home to Newport County Martin Harvey was sacked. That was an eye-opener for me. The day after the Newport game the entire team was invited to the Chairman's home. We thought it was all to do with boosting morale. But the next morning I went into the ground and learned that Martin had been sacked. I remember thinking: 'There's no justice in this game.' The players felt Martin had done a good job and it was just a matter of time before we started to get results again. John Pickering, who'd been brought in to look after the coaching, had worked hard with the players and felt as bad as the rest of us.

The following day we learned that Bob Stokoe had been appointed manager as Martin's replacement. That seemed rather hasty to most of us and it looked as though there'd been something going on behind the scenes for several days.

That probably heralded my worst period at Carlisle. Bob Stokoe went for experience to start with and I found myself struggling to get into the team. Some weeks I was in but more often I was a substitute. The bad run continued and I remember playing one disastrous game at home to Chesterfield which we lost 6–2. Arthur Cox was the Chesterfield manager at the time. He later became my manager at Newcastle and ironically had worked with Bob Stokoe at Sunderland when they won the Cup in 1973.

Bob had brought in Dick Young as one of his coaches and he used to give me a hard time in training. I still had more than three years of my contract to go and there were occasional moments when I thought I'd never survive another week let alone the full three years, but gradually things improved and our results started to pick up. The club signed Bryan Robson, who'd been a big favourite of mine when he played for Newcastle. Pop, as he was known, was still a tremendous player and his experience rubbed off on the rest of the team.

It was around this time that I got my first car. One of the local garages decided to sponsor the club and offered three sponsored cars for the players. It was a good deal. They were offering a brand new car for which you paid a minimal weekly rent of about £10. Jimmy Hamilton and Bobby Parker had one each while Paul Bannon, Andy Collins and I argued over the remaining one. The only problem was that none of us could drive. I was having a lesson every three or four weeks and couldn't afford to take any more. Then, out of the blue, a businessman offered to sponsor me and the car. He paid £100 for me to take extra driving lessons, so I changed instructors and went on an intensive course taking three or four hour long lessons a day. I took my test within a few weeks and passed first time.

The car was mine, but by then the businessman had changed his mind about the sponsorship deal and had decided he didn't want his name on the side of the car. So I had a brand new car – a Fiat Mirafiori, registration number KRM 63W – with my name on the side. I was still only 18 but I felt great, as though I'd really made it. In the days when I was on the dole owning a car seemed a long way off. I couldn't wait to go home to Newcastle to show it off to all my mates. It cost me just £10 a week, and I've never met the man who paid for me to get through the test.

It was through Carlisle that I met the woman who was to become my wife. I'd always been shy with girls but I'd taken a particular fancy to one who worked in the club's main office. The lads told me she was called Sandra and it soon became obvious that I had a soft spot for her. I used to pop into the office at every opportunity, to borrow a pen, ask the time, check if there were any messages and all the normal excuses. The lads were always taking the mickey and teasing me but I was too scared to ask her out.

I was still sharing digs with Stan, and because he was an apprentice he had to do jobs like cleaning the boots and sweeping the changing rooms. So, when all the other lads had gone, I'd wait in the main office, hoping to chat to Sandra until Stan had finished. Eventually I plucked up the courage to ask her out, and to my amazement she said yes.

I didn't have the car at the time but Mick McCartney and his wife offered to take us out for our first date to help the romance get started. We went to the String of Horses at Faugh, just outside Carlisle. I really enjoyed myself, had scampi and chips and felt really proud. Sandra and I got on incredibly well and our romance blossomed.

Her family were marvellous. I was having trouble finding good digs so they invited me round for a meal every night. Before long Sandra and I were engaged and fixed a date for our wedding the following year. But within weeks those plans were thrown into disarray as my career took an exciting new twist.

My second season with Carlisle had improved after those early doubts following Martin Harvey's departure. I regained a regular place in the team and Bob Stokoe encouraged me to play behind the centre-forward. He wanted me to link midfield with attack and run from deep, taking players on so defenders would be pulled out of position. It suited my game and I scored 15 goals that season.

I'd read in the papers that Vancouver Whitecaps were interested in signing me but dismissed it as paper talk, just a story to fill in on a thin day. We'd heard that a scout from Vancouver had been to Brunton Park to watch a Mansfield player in an FA Cup second round replay on a cold, damp and extremely foggy Cumbrian winter's evening. I thought I'd played reasonably well that night but I certainly wasn't outstanding, and when someone else said that Vancouver were interested I thought they must have got the wrong player; after all it had been misty and it was difficult to see some parts of the pitch.

A few months later Johnny Giles, who was the Vancouver manager, turned up to watch our game away to Brentford. Ron Harris was in the Brentford team that day. I'd obviously heard about his reputation, and although he wasn't marking me there were times when he came close to giving me a good kicking. Luckily my speed kept me out of trouble and we came away with a 1–1 draw after a good game.

The newspapers were now suggesting that Vancouver were interested in signing our goalkeeper, Trevor Swinburne, and my name seemed to have disappeared out of the frame. Then Bob

Stokoe called me into his office one morning and said: 'Vancouver want to sign you. I think it would be a good move.'

My first reaction was: 'Where's Vancouver?' I thought it was in the United States and had no idea it was in Canada. After looking it up in the atlas I met the Whitecaps president Peter Bridgewater who painted a marvellous picture of life over there. The deal included free air tickets for my parents to come and see me during the summer but I still had doubts about going alone.

Apart from a weekend football trip to Holland, I'd never been abroad before, but this seemed to be a great opportunity. And they would let me return to play for Carlisle the following winter. I went into the next room to discuss it with Sandra.

She said: 'It's up to you. If you want to go, then go.' I said I didn't want to go on my own so I suggested that we bring the wedding forward so she could come as well. She gulped and then agreed, and within three weeks we were married and on the plane to Canada.

Those three weeks were the most hectic of my life. I was still training and playing with Carlisle but luckily Sandra's mum organised the wedding. All I had to do was turn up. She even arranged my wedding suit. The day before the wedding we played Burnley away and won 3–0. Gordon Staniforth, who was my best-man, scored a hat-trick that night. I was given the Wednesday off to get married but was back for training on the Thursday afternoon. Two days later I played my last game of the season at home to Charlton. We lost 2–1. That night I packed my bags, and 12 hours later Sandra and I set off for our new life in Vancouver.

4
VANCOUVER

Before I left England the newspapers were carrying stories advising me not to go to Canada. Bobby Moncur and Arthur Cox were both quoted as saying it would be a mistake, and others were suggesting it was foolish to play in a league which many people in Britain didn't take seriously.

The North American Soccer League (NASL) had introduced some of its own rules, like the 35-yard off-side line, and was heading for a dispute with FIFA, the sport's governing body, which could have led to North America being outcast from world soccer. But I'd spoken to others, including Pop Robson, who'd said it was a great opportunity. He said that if I didn't go I would probably regret it in a few years time. And if it was good enough for players like Johnny Giles, Peter Lorimer, Dave Thomas and Terry Yorath there couldn't be much wrong with it.

That journey to Vancouver was the first time that either Sandra or I had flown. I'd previously thought a trip to Darlington was an adventure, now I was going half way round the world.

I soon discovered that life in Vancouver was very different from what I'd been used to in England. In the North-East in particular jobs were scarce and people seemed to be under pressure to get enough money just to survive. But in Vancouver there were plenty of jobs, mostly well paid, and people seemed relaxed and quite affluent.

The club found Sandra and me a flat, they provided us with a car and we soon settled in. There were a few Canadians in the Vancouver Whitecaps team but it was mainly made up of players from the British Isles. The defence included Jimmy Holmes, Roger Kenyon and Pierce O'Leary. Peter Lorimer still played and the forward line included Ray Hankin and Alan Taylor.

Johnny Giles ran the team as though it was an English club so we were spared some of the more eccentric razzmatazz common among some of the other North American clubs. And I soon found that the League was every bit as serious and competitive as the Football League in England. There were, however, still a number of differences from what I'd been used to at Carlisle. For a start we played in a huge, all-seater stadium and the pitch was plastic. It was more like a household carpet than some of the artificial pitches that have since been introduced in England, and before each game the groundstaff would soak it to make the bounce more even. I'd worried about playing on astroturf but soon adapted and found that the smooth and even surface suited my sort of game.

The changing rooms were enormous by English League standards. The clubs were used to American-football teams who need space for 40 or so players to get changed. They were so large that in some rooms you could quite easily have played a five-a-side game.

In England, clubs like Hartlepool and Colchester didn't have the money to spend on fancy facilities and the changing rooms were generally darker and dirtier. Once you got the team in, that was it. There often wasn't enough room to swing your arms up to pull on a shirt, and after the game you'd often have to queue for the one shower that was working. By the time the last person got in there'd be no more hot water.

But everything at Vancouver was bigger, brighter and better. The training facilities were marvellous and the medical facilities were excellent with all the latest equipment. If you picked up a knock in England you'd go to a physio room where there would be a chair, a desk and a couch. In Vancouver the couch was like a hospital bed and the room had every modern medical machine you could want.

Sandra and I settled easily into our new life. We made a number of good friends. Barry Siddall, the former Sunderland goalkeeper, joined Vancouver shortly after me and moved into the same apartment block. His wife was from the North-East, and, like us, she'd never been so far from home before. I also became good friends with Dave Thomas. He was another North-East lad and had a similar temperament to me. We were both home-loving lads and couldn't believe that we were being paid to travel around North America and play football.

Sandra had completed a business studies course concentrating on football administration before she started work at Carlisle and she spent some time in the Vancouver office learning about the different techniques on the other side of the Atlantic. Dave Thomas's wife, Brenda, was fully aware of the problems of living in a country where you didn't know anybody and befriended us and made sure we didn't get homesick. When I went off on away trips I knew Sandra had someone to be with. Being newly married I was especially concerned that Sandra should be happy, and knowing she was with Brenda meant I didn't have to worry about her feeling lonely and miserable.

The size of my transfer fee had surprised many people. Vancouver had paid Carlisle more than £250,000 when they bought me. I'm sure the Canadian fans wondered why the Whitecaps had spent so much money on an unknown player from the English Third Division. I was flattered that anyone could think I was worth so much and it was a great boost to my confidence that Vancouver were prepared to gamble so much money on someone who was relatively inexperienced.

There was plenty of publicity about my arrival. The Canadians are much more media conscious than English clubs. At Vancouver every player was given a number which he kept throughout the season. Players didn't change numbers from game to game as they do in England. And the numbers bore no relation to the position, as they do in the traditional numbering systems at home, so teams rarely took the field with players wearing the numbers 1 to 11.

When I arrived most of the numbers had been taken and I had a choice of something in the high 20s or number 13. It seemed nobody had wanted the burden of wearing the unlucky number. That old superstition didn't bother me so I said 'I'll wear 13 then.' The publicity man started dancing for joy. 'That's brilliant!' he said. 'What a great story for the papers: "Whitecaps Star goes for Lucky 13". They'll love it.' I can't remember whether any of the newspapers shared his enthusiasm for the story but I know that number 13 worked well enough for me in my time in Canada.

Luckily the crowd took to me early on. When the team came out for a match the players were announced one by one. When the public address system boomed out your name, you ran out to the centre-circle. Then the next player would be announced and he'd run out and so on.

Because I played up front I was always the last man out and always given a tremendous reception by the crowd. It's impossible to explain how much that means to a player. If you know the crowd are behind you it gives you that extra confidence to try things you might otherwise be scared of.

My first game was against the Seattle Sounders. That was considered a local derby – Seattle is only 130 miles from Vancouver – and after we'd lost a keenly contested match 3–2 I was given a surprising introduction to the different relationship between football clubs and the media in Canada. I came off the pitch to find the dressing room packed full of people. I hadn't been at the club long enough to know who was who, so I just assumed that the board of directors had come in early.

Suddenly a man appeared at my side, pushed a microphone under my nose, looked towards a camera and started shouting at me: 'What did you think of your first game?'

I wondered what was going on. It didn't occur to me that we could be on television. In England, all the interviews were done well after the game when you'd changed and showered. They were never conducted in the dressing room.

This fellow asked his question again, but I still hadn't realised what was happening, even though there were television lights glaring in my face. I slowly took my shirt off and said: 'What do you mean, what do I think?'

By now this reporter must have been convinced that he was in the middle of what would go down as one of his most disastrous interviews but he asked his question again. I looked round for one of the lads to explain what was going on, but they were all talking so I came out with the normal platitudes about it being a good game, disappointing to lose and hoping to win next time, and could see the other lads laughing. I was convinced they were winding me up.

The reporter thanked me and moved on to the next player. I asked someone what was going on and it was only then that they told me I'd been on live television. I must have looked a right idiot.

Most of our matches were televised, especially when we played away. But the Canadian programme schedulers had little under-standing when it came to football. At frequent intervals during the game they would cut away from the action to show the adverts. If a goal was scored during that time it was too bad. After the adverts they returned to the game and the commentator would announce that while they'd been away Vancouver had scored a great goal. They never showed a replay until the end of the game so the viewer was never sure what had happened.

It was also the first time I had seen myself on television. Border Television sometimes used to show a minute's worth of highlights from Carlisle games on their local news programmes, but in Canada I had the chance to see for myself what I was doing wrong during a game.

One thing I found strange was adjusting to the irregular pattern of our fixture list. In England I was used to everyone playing their games on a Saturday. In America you were never sure when you would play. It was very rare for the whole League to play on the same day, and some weeks we'd play on a Sunday, others a Tuesday and another on a Friday. There was no regular day for Whitecaps games and it was never the same from one week to the next.

We travelled all over North America for our away games. Whereas at Carlisle I'd had to get used to long coach journeys when we played away I now had to get used to long flights. The club tried to arrange to play three or four away games over a ten day period to minimise the travelling. We would fly to New York for the first game, then down to Dallas for the second and on to Florida for our third match before flying home to Vancouver.

It was better than being on holiday. I was away with a group of friends, seeing America and having a great adventure. The club would hire four huge station wagons rather than travel by coach. The management team which included Johnny Giles, Peter Lorimer and George Wright would go in one and the players would divide up into the other three.

In my second season I landed a job as one of the drivers. I loved it, driving down a five-lane highway in an enormous car and taking in the vastness of the country. I saw more of America that way than if I'd been stuck in a coach.

It was on these away trips that I first came across the American razzmatazz that people associate with soccer in the States. We played Dallas Tornadoes who'd borrowed the cheerleaders from the Dallas Cowboys American-football team. I'd never seen anything like it. The girls danced up and down the side of the pitch throughout the entire game. There was something strange about running down the wing, with the sound of a grunting defender in one ear and a group of cheerleaders singing in the other. I couldn't imagine that catching on in places like Rotherham or Grimsby.

The crowds didn't need much encouragement to get excited. There were none of the chants that I'd been used to in England but there was always a good atmosphere. The Vancouver crowd originated what became known during the 1986 World Cup as the Mexican Wave. It began in the Empire Stadium. A man would appear behind the goal with a huge cue card which read: 'Oggi, oggi, oggi'. The crowd behind the goal would stand up, shout the words and wave their arms, and as soon as they'd finished a man would hold a huge cue card up at the other end which read: 'Oy! oy! oy!' and the crowd down there would be out of their seats and shouting. This seemed to go on for ages and it made a tremendous noise.

The Canadians would cheer things which no English crowd would ever get excited about, like a throw in. And we had to play to the accompaniment of a commentator telling the story of the game over the public address system. 'It's a corner to the Whitecaps,' he used to boom as you came up to take the kick.

The Vancouver team had its own wacky figures. None were zanier than Tino Lettieri who was in goal for the Whitecaps during my last season with the club and went on to play for Canada in the 1986 World Cup finals in Mexico. He was an Italian Canadian and a great character. Most goalkeepers are mad but Tino was nuttier than any I've ever met. He loved to entertain the crowd and was even more eccentric than Bruce Grobbelaar, who'd played for the Whitecaps three or four years earlier.

Tino loved parrots. He kept some at home and used to bring along a toy parrot on match days which he would put down in the back of his net along with his gloves and goalkeeper's bag.

The fans loved this gimmick but the parrot's greatest moment came in a game against the San Diego Sockers. The referee gave a penalty against us after Tino fouled one of the San Diego forwards. Tino didn't agree with the decision and went berserk. He argued

29

the point with the referee and when the ref refused to change his mind Tino said: 'Right. That's it. I'm not going in goal.'

Instead he collected his parrot from the back of the net, placed it carefully on the line in the centre of the goal and walked off towards the edge of the area.

'There you go,' he said. 'Have your shot. I'm not going in goal so the parrot will have to save the penalty.' The crowd loved it.

At the end of the game I thought Tino's behaviour would land him in trouble. But when we got to the changing room the chairman had sent down a dozen bottles of champagne. He'd realised that the fans had enjoyed Tino's antics and would be talking about it for weeks. They'd probably be back to see what he got up to next time.

By the next game the parrot gimmick was getting out of hand. Tino arranged for an actor to dress up as a parrot and dance around behind the goal. Every time the opposition attacked the man-sized parrot would dive around behind Tino. It was obviously a distraction and whenever the opposition got in our half the parrot would do all kinds of stupid things. The referee started to lose his patience but he didn't know what to do.

At half-time we went off and passed a man in a gorilla suit in the tunnel. He was making his way onto the pitch carrying a large stuffed toy which was dressed in a referee's kit. The gorilla went onto the centre-circle and entertained the crowd during half-time by beating up this model referee. The crowd loved it, especially as the match referee had annoyed them by not seeing the funny side of Tino's life-size parrot.

Tino had started a craze and started to market replicas of his toy parrot. He made a nice profit. They were snapped up and within a month we could see everyone in the crowd was waving one of Tino's toys.

You never knew what Tino would do next. In one game he clashed with Adi Coker, who used to play for West Ham. Adi was having a bad time and we could see he was getting worked up. One of his team-mates had already been sent off and eventually Adi lost his cool and he was sent off as well.

Tino went to his bag, produced a toy machine gun and started chasing Coker off the pitch, pretending to shoot him. Once again the crowd loved it and once again Tino received another 12 bottles of champagne from the chairman.

Tino's antics were the exception in North America – he was the League's eccentric figure – and although there were some crazy moments the games were very competitive and taken as seriously as football anywhere in the world. The standard of football was higher than I'd been used to in the Third Division with Carlisle. Vancouver were one of the top three teams in the North American Soccer League. If they'd played in England they would have probably been a mid-table First Division side comparable to teams like Southampton or Coventry.

New York Cosmos and Chicago Stings were the main rivals. The other teams were of a similar standard to those clubs at the bottom of the First Division or top of the Second. The six or seven teams at the bottom of the NASL were never likely to win the League but were always capable of upsetting the top clubs. Out of 30 League games we expected to win between 20 and 22 each season, and although we never won the League when I was there we were always in the end of season championship play-offs.

There were never any drawn games in America. If the scores were level after 90 minutes the game went into overtime, which was seven and a half minutes each way, but it was also sudden death so the first team to score were the winners. If the scores were still level after overtime, the game then went to a shoot-out. This was marvellous for the fans but not all the players relished it.

It was one against one. The attacker started with the ball on the 35-yard line and had five seconds to score with only the opposing goalkeeper to beat. Each team nominated five players and, if the scores were still level after their efforts, then it was sudden death and the rest of the team would have a go. Occasionally you'd have goalkeeper taking on goalkeeper.

I enjoyed the shoot-out. If you scored you became a hero. My tactics depended on who was in goal for the opposition. Because so many games were televised, we were able to study what other teams did in the shoot-out. Some keepers would stay on their line and others would come charging out. Having watched them on TV you knew what to expect.

I preferred facing the goalkeepers who stayed on their line. You could run right up to them and tuck the ball into the corner of the net. More difficult were the goalkeepers who rushed out. I used to knock the ball forward to the edge of the penalty area and assess the situation from there.

Sometimes you could chip the keeper, other times you could go round him but to add to the pressure there was a clock behind the goal reminding you that you only had five seconds. The crowd would build up the tension by counting down, 5–4–3–2–1! You dreaded hearing the sound of the buzzer which signalled your time was up.

I learned a lot from my time with Vancouver. Johnny Giles was a marvellous manager and an excellent coach. He taught me to relax when I was on the ball. At Carlisle I'd felt that everything I did had to result in a goal but Johnny made me appreciate other aspects of the game and improved my vision and awareness of what was happening around me.

But most of all Johnny was honest with his players. I remember one game where he substituted me before half-time. We were playing Seattle and struggling because of injuries. I'd been up against Kenny Hibbit and thought I was doing quite well. But Kenny was more experienced than me and was using a few tricks to exploit my naivety. He had me running all over the place and I was exhausted when I was pulled off but still annoyed to have been substituted with so long to go.

But at half-time Johnny came straight over and explained. 'You were trying so hard son but you're having a nightmare. Your touch isn't there, which can happen to all of us but you're having such a bad game I feel sorry for you.'

We were losing 1–0 when I came off and the team went on to win without me. Johnny could have given me a fancy story about trying a different formation, but he chose to be honest and I respected him for that. That way you know where you stand. He was very good about it and I realised that just because I was working hard it didn't mean I was playing well. Above all, that incident taught me to be more self-critical.

Some people have said that I wasted three years by playing in North America but I don't see it that way. I enjoyed my football and learned from players who'd been the best and had invaluable experience of playing football at the highest level. I'd seen life in a different country, which always makes you a more understanding person. I was also lucky enough to win the player of the year award in my first year; I shared the award with Peter Lorimer in my second year; and won it outright again in my last season. That was a tremendous honour, and in my final season the fans voted me the most popular player.

I played in some marvellous grounds. While I was there, Vancouver moved to a new 60,000 capacity, all-seater, covered stadium. There wasn't a bad seat in the ground, there were no pillars obstructing the view and it was the best stadium I'd ever played in, until I played at Wembley.

Our first game there was against Seattle and it was a sell-out. The Seattle team included several British players, including Joe Corrigan, Ray Evans, Peter Ward, Alan Hudson and Steve Daley and they threatened to spoil our party by taking the lead. But just when it looked as though our big day would finish on a low note I managed to score two second-half goals to help us come back and win 2–1. The place erupted. I've never heard a noise like it. All 60,000 Vancouver fans were on their feet and the roof made the noise sound even louder.

There are a number of lessons the English game could learn from America. The off-side law in the NASL was a vast improvement on what we are used to at home, where a player can be off-side anywhere inside his opponents' half. In America the off-side law only operated in the area 35 yards from goal. The British game suffers from too many teams who play the off-side trap, with defenders pushing up to the half-way line and squashing play into a restricted area. It spoils the game, it's boring for spectators and it's frustrating for most of the players. If both teams push up the game is suffocated but that could be avoided by introducing the 35-yard rule and opening up more space for the midfield.

There were several other more zany suggestions to 'improve' the game. One man wanted to make the goals larger to encourage high scoring games. He said the dimensions of the present goals – eight yards wide by eight feet tall – were introduced the previous century when people were generally shorter. Now goalkeepers were taller he thought it fair to make the goals bigger!

There was some talk of abandoning the system of playing 45 minutes each way and introducing three periods of 30 minutes each. This was suggested by television companies who wanted more breaks in the play to give them more time for their lucrative advertisements.

33

But unfortunately interest in professional soccer in North America was dwindling by the time I left Vancouver. The Whitecaps were still attracting crowds of 25,000 to 30,000, but a number of other clubs folded and the League was reduced to just a handful of teams. In four years it shrank from 24 clubs to just seven, with five clubs closing in 1981 alone. Two years later Seattle Sounders closed. At their peak they'd attracted crowds of around 60,000 but interest there had faded. I think one of the main reasons was that only a few of the players were natives. The rest were foreigners and often they were in the twilight of their careers and more interested in making some easy money than training hard.

And of course players who were big names in Europe were unknown when they went to America. Johnny Giles, Peter Lorimer and Terry Yorath were household names in England, the sort the crowds would love to see, but nobody knew of them in Dallas or Florida. Canada and the United States needed to produce their own stars.

But although attendances fell there is still a tremendous amount of interest in football. It's popular in the schools and I'm sure that by the end of the century, when the next couple of generations of American soccer players have grown up, football will be one of the major sports in the United States. The decision to hold the 1994 World Cup there could be just the boost the sport needs to get equal attention with baseball and American football. It's the big chance for the game to take off and by that time they will have produced their own stars, the crowds who go to watch them will understand the game, and they'll go on to produce a team of world beaters.

5
MANCHESTER UNITED

I'm sure every player would love the chance to play for a big club like Manchester United. I was no exception and when the opportunity came I set off for Old Trafford full of hope and anticipation of what was to come. Six months later I left feeling disappointed and frustrated that I'd never been given a chance to show what I could do.

It all started off so well. Manchester United came to Canada for a close-season tour which included a game against Vancouver Whitecaps. We beat them 3–1 and I scored twice. The first goal was after just 13 seconds. They kicked off and almost immediately Terry Yorath tackled Gordon McQueen, the United centre-half. Terry knocked the ball to me and I hit a left-foot shot into the corner.

In the second half I scored again. A ball was played to me down the inside-right channel. I had my back to goal, controlled the ball with the outside of my right foot, turned inside and struck another left-foot shot which went into the top corner. It seemed as though I could do nothing wrong in that game. Obviously I was very excited to have scored, especially against a Manchester United side that included many of their big stars.

After the match the United manager, Ron Atkinson, spoke to my boss Johnny Giles about taking me to Old Trafford for the winter to see how things went. It was too good an opportunity to miss. I'd always liked Manchester United and had grown up admiring players like George Best. They had such a fine tradition of turning out good teams and were undoubtedly one of the top clubs in Europe, perhaps even the world.

I'd already made up my mind before I asked Johnny Giles for his advice. He urged me to make the most of the opportunity. 'Enjoy it,' he said. 'Don't worry about anything else like money, just make sure it goes well.'

So Sandra and I flew back to England for the start of what we hoped would be a long and fruitful career with Manchester United. Everything about the club was impressive. When I signed, Martin Edwards, the chairman, brought along a bottle of the club's own label champagne. That evening I watched the first team beat Everton 2–1 with goals from Norman Whiteside and Bryan Robson in front of a crowd of more than 43,000.

The papers all carried stories about me joining United and all raised the same question: 'Will Beardsley get in the team?' I played in a similar position to Norman Whiteside and it seemed that he was set to become the first choice. Norman had come through the club's junior and reserve sides. He was still only 17 years old but had just returned from the 1982 World Cup in Spain where he'd made a good impression and was one of the reasons behind the Northern Ireland team's success. In that first game I could see for myself that he was a good player.

I'd heard a great deal about Old Trafford but the day I signed was the first time I'd ever been there. You can't help but be impressed. The stadium is one of the best in Europe and I couldn't wait to play there for the first team.

The club paid for Sandra and I to stay in a hotel before they gave us a club flat in Chorlton-cum-Hardy, which wasn't too far from the ground. Bryan Robson had lived there before us and after several weeks in a hotel it was great to have somewhere we could call home. The club sponsors, Sharp, even provided us with a colour television.

No-one was more excited about the move than my brother-in-law, Sean. He was only 14 years old at the time and was a United fanatic. He was so devoted that when I got him free tickets for the seats he turned them down because he'd rather pay and stand in the Stretford End.

Although I was excited about the move, to begin with I was a little apprehensive about joining such a famous club. When I arrived I was put straight into the first-team changing room at the

Cliff, the club's training ground. That was unusual. Unless they were established stars, the new players would normally change with the reserves. I found myself in the same changing room as England internationals like Bryan Robson, Steve Coppell and Ray Wilkins and, to be honest, I was a little in awe of them.

I became good friends with Mike Duxbury. We were the first two to arrive for training each morning and had time to chat and read through the papers together.

Mike had recently broken through to the first team. He'd started as a triallist and worked his way up through the youth squad and reserves so he understood what it was like for players who weren't part of the first team set up. He could sense that I felt overawed but kept telling me not to worry.

Although I changed with the first team at the Cliff, I was training and playing with the reserves. The reserve team included Mark Hughes and Paul McGrath, who both went on to become first-team regulars, and both Arnold Muhren and Ray Wilkins played for us when they were coming back from injury.

Brian Whitehouse was in charge and believed that the basis for his training sessions should be plenty of running. He concentrated almost exclusively on stamina work. I'd played football for more than two and a half years non-stop and didn't really need to work on my fitness or my stamina. I knew I was fit. What I needed was the chance to build up my experience by playing with top quality players. To make matters worse, while we were running I could see the first-team squad doing plenty of ball-work and playing five-a-side games.

I was desperate to see more of the ball in training so I could show what I could do. I could hardly expect Brian Whitehouse to change his entire routine for me so I went to see Ron Atkinson to ask if I could train with the first team. After all, Ron had spent more than a quarter of a million pounds on me and I thought he might like to see what he'd got for his money.

But Ron said he wanted to keep his first-team squad of 13 or 14 players separate and he didn't have room for me.

'That's the way I am,' he said. 'If you can break in, good for you. If not then you'll have to persevere in the reserves.'

So I kept doing my best in the second team and waited for my chance. It came on 6 October 1982. The previous Saturday I scored a hat-trick against Stoke Reserves in the Central League.

That performance earned me my call up to the first team for the Milk Cup tie at home to Bournemouth. They were in the Third Division and only 22,000 turned up to watch the game, the lowest crowd of the season at Old Trafford.

It was my big moment but I didn't even last the full 90 minutes. Ron Atkinson pulled me off and sent on Norman Whiteside in my place. I was bitterly disappointed. We won the game 2–0 and I thought I'd played quite well considering it was my first game. I'd even been close to scoring our first goal. I was unmarked on the far post and ideally placed to touch home a cross as it came across the Bournemouth goal. But Bournemouth's Harry Redknapp just got a touch before me to put it in his own net, so it was credited as an own goal.

I often wonder what would have happened had Harry missed the ball and I had scored. My career could have taken a completely different turn. I might have stayed on for the rest of the game, made another couple of appearances and established myself in the United team.

But it wasn't to be. The following Saturday I was named as substitute for the first-team game against Stoke. The game was still goalless and I'd sat on the bench for more than an hour before Ron Atkinson told me to start warming up. 'Great,' I thought, 'I'm going to get a game.' I went through my stretching exercises conscientiously for seven or eight minutes. I was itching to get on when suddenly Bryan Robson scored to put United ahead. Ron leaned out of the dug-out and said: 'You might as well sit down son, there's no need for you to go on now.'

So that hour or so against Bournemouth was my first and last game for the United first team, and the following week I was back in the reserves.

The first-team players had been marvellous to me. I'd played alongside Frank Stapleton against Bournemouth and afterwards he came up and apologised for not helping me. 'I should have done more,' he said, 'I'm sorry.' It wasn't necessary. Frank had laid off some lovely balls for me and it had been a joy to play in the same team as him.

But now I was back in the reserves and trying to motivate myself, playing in empty grounds, where every shout echoed around the deserted terraces. Manchester United reserves attracted quite large crowds by second-team standards. If those crowds were packed into a compact Fourth Division ground they might create some sort of atmosphere but even 2–3000 are lost in a vast stadium like Old Trafford.

The club would only open one stand for reserve matches so three sides of the ground were deserted. When you ran down the wing alongside one of the empty stands there was nothing but an eerie echo. It was difficult for players to get fired up and the games often felt like practise matches rather than serious competition.

What made it harder was that nobody seemed to be bothered about the reserves. Ron Atkinson rarely came to see us play and we got the impression that as long as the first team were doing well then the club was OK. Nothing else seemed to matter.

I could see the manager's point of view. His job depends on the success of the first team. If they keep losing it's no use him saying: 'Well the reserves are having a good run.' The supporters are mainly interested in the first team results but that's little consolation to the players working hard and giving everything week after week in the second team. We all wanted the manager to be interested in what we were doing but he didn't take any notice.

It wasn't so bad for me. Under the terms of the transfer I could go back to Vancouver if things didn't work out with United. At least I had some security and another option if I didn't make it there, but some of the other lads were trying so hard week after week never knowing when, or even if, an opportunity would come their way. They had no idea what the future held and could do no more than hope for a lucky break.

Reserve team players can easily feel like outsiders. Everything centres around the first team and it's easy for the reserves to feel left out. It's not that the first-team players look down on the reserves but the spotlight automatically falls on the stars. Consequently they have the confidence to mess about and have a joke while the reserves, and especially the new players, hold back and feel uncomfortable about joining in.

I was shy anyway and there were plenty of times when I didn't feel involved, more through my fault than anybody else's. I was happy to be in the company of world class players and quite content to sit quietly and take everything in.

The first-team players were very good towards me. Bryan Robson was very friendly and I was impressed with Ray Wilkins,

who was the club captain when I arrived. He realised the import-
ance of keeping up morale throughout the club. Every morning he
would go into the first-team changing room to get ready for
training and then go and chat to the reserves and the apprentices.
There was no need for him to do that but it made everyone feel part
of the club.

Ray went out of his way to help me settle. He realised that
Sandra and I didn't know anyone so whenever there was a party or
a reception he would pick us up and drive us there. Again it was a
nice gesture and I can't speak highly enough of Ray both as a
footballer and a friend.

He went through a disappointing season after breaking his
cheekbone. He was out for several weeks, and during his comeback
I played alongside him in the reserves. He was a class above
everyone else and brought out the best in the players around him.
He thinks about the game, has some great ideas and is good
at handling players. I'm sure that one day Ray will make a
marvellous manager.

But as much as I enjoyed being associated with Manchester
United I didn't feel that I was going anywhere. For all the running
I was doing in training it seemed that my career was standing still.
I was 21 years old and my next step should have been into the First
Division. Having been a first-team regular at Vancouver it was a
backward step to drop into the reserves at Manchester United.
And there seemed little prospect of me ever breaking into the
United first team.

Vancouver had agreed that if Manchester United didn't want
me I would go back to Canada, and United would get their money
back. Ron Atkinson was supposed to make up his mind towards
the end of the season but by Christmas it seemed obvious to me
that I wasn't going to be asked to stay on. I continued playing for
the reserves, hoping for a chance, but by February it seemed more
remote than ever.

I went to see Ron Atkinson and he agreed that I could go back
early. I was disappointed that United were letting me go. I'd been
desperate for a chance to prove that I could play in the First
Division but I thought it would be better to return to Vancouver,
where I knew I was wanted, than stay at Old Trafford where I
could spend another couple of years in the reserves before maybe
drifting to a club in the lower divisions.

Surprisingly I felt happier once everything was sorted out. Sandra and I had spent the previous six months living in limbo, uncertain whether to look for a home around Manchester or start making plans for a return to Canada.

Looking back I can see why Ron Atkinson let me go. United won the FA Cup that season after beating Brighton in the final, they were runners-up in the Milk Cup after losing to Liverpool in the final, and finished third in the League. That's a fair season by anyone's standards.

But Ron also had an abundance of talent at the club at that time. Norman Whiteside was playing in the role I had hoped to fill alongside Frank Stapleton, and Mark Hughes was starting to push for a place in the first team.

Norman was only 17 but it was obvious that he had a great future ahead of him. He was big and strong even then. It was impossible to knock him off the ball. Other lads of that age would need a rest from the demands of professional football but Norman was able to carry on all season.

He scored a brilliant goal for United in the Milk Cup final that season. He received the ball with his back to goal and was closely marked by Liverpool's Alan Hansen. Somehow he turned Alan and drove his shot into the corner. It was hard to believe that he was so young but he was always a confident lad. People talked about him being the new George Best, which is a heavy burden to hang around a young player. But Norman coped with the pressure without any problems.

In those days he was very competitive, even in training. He was obviously out to make his mark and left a few bruises on the way. But once he'd established a regular place in the first team he started to save his energy for match days and was a lot less rough in training.

It was obvious that Mark Hughes was going to be good. He was single-minded in the way that all the best strikers are and he had the ability and strength to hold the ball and roll his man. He was an excellent trainer and looked to have the potential to become a great player.

Ron Atkinson obviously felt he was adequately covered with those two and I'm in no position to argue. Norman became a regular in the first team and a hero at Old Trafford. Mark Hughes made a terrific impact in the First Division before United sold him to Barcelona for £2 million. Mark had come through the ranks so the £2 million was all profit and good business from United's point of view. Not many clubs can boast a profit like that on one player. Of course the only problem is that the fans often don't want to see the best players leave no matter how much the club sells them for.

But at the time I was upset that Ron offered no explanation when he let me go. That hurt. And I also felt that I hadn't been given a chance to show what I could do. If I'd been given the chance to train with the first team he could at least have seen how I could play.

Although my time at Old Trafford ended in disappointment I don't regret my six months there. It was a great experience to be part of a big club and to mix with so many world class players. And I learnt not to worry when things weren't going my way.

In the past I'd been hurt when clubs like Gillingham and Cambridge had rejected me, and at the time it was only the support of my family that kept me going. But now I'd matured and had faith in my ability despite the temporary blow to my confidence.

Deep down I always felt that I would play in the First Division one day. I'd taken so many setbacks in the past that I knew I shouldn't let people put me down. And I was learning that if you want something badly enough you should keep fighting for it. I flew back across the Atlantic more determined than ever to show Manchester United they were wrong to let me go.

6
GOING HOME

After the frustration and disappointment of my six months with Manchester United I couldn't wait to get back to Vancouver and play first-team football again.

I was lucky to be able to go back to such a good club. Johnny Giles was very understanding. He was sure that I'd get another chance in England and quickly helped to rebuild my confidence. When I left United, Johnny told me to take a couple of weeks' holiday before I started training with Vancouver once more. Sandra and I went to Florida. It was my first break from football for three years and the first time Sandra and I had been on holiday. It worked wonders. I went back to Vancouver fully refreshed and raring to go.

We had a successful season – my best in Canada. We finished top of the League after winning 24 out of 30 League games. Only two or three of those went to shoot-outs. But then we lost in the first round of the play-offs. As we had finished top we played the team that finished eighth, Toronto. The ties were settled over three games. They beat us 1–0 in the final game in Vancouver to knock us out.

That was my last game in Canada. My contract had run its full three years, and although Johnny Giles offered me a new one he was quite candid when he said he wasn't sure that the North American Soccer League would survive another season. Vancouver were still a healthy club but others were in financial difficulty and looked set to drop out of the League.

Johnny also explained that Newcastle United had been on the

43

phone to make an enquiry about signing me. When I was at Carlisle there were reports that Newcastle had wanted to sign me although nothing came of it then. But now it seemed Arthur Cox, the Newcastle manager, was making a firm bid.

It was a dream come true. Newcastle were my local team. I'd supported them since I was a boy and had always hoped that I'd one day get the chance to wear the famous black and white shirt. I spoke to Arthur Cox on the phone and agreed to sign immediately. I couldn't wait to get home.

And there was the added attraction of playing in the same side as Kevin Keegan. I remember hearing the news that Keegan had signed for Newcastle the previous year. I'd gone shopping in Vancouver with Sandra. She'd popped into one of the stores while I sat in the car listening to the radio news. The final story took me completely by surprise.

'The English soccer club Newcastle United have pulled off a major coup by signing Kevin Keegan ... ,' announced the newsreader. I thought they must have made a mistake. The story was probably written by someone who didn't understand football and they'd got it wrong. I told Sandra and she laughed but that night it was in all the papers and I started to believe it was true.

Newcastle just missed out on promotion from Division Two in Keegan's first season at St James's Park. Queen's Park Rangers, Wolves and Leicester had gone up, Fulham were fourth, and Newcastle finished in fifth place.

But Keegan's arrival had generated renewed interest and enthusiasm for football in the North-East. More than 500,000 people watched Newcastle's home games that season, and their average gate, more than 24,000, was easily the best in the Second Division and better than all but four clubs in the First Division.

If I hadn't been going home to Newcastle it would have been hard to leave Vancouver. We'd enjoyed a fantastic lifestyle with a lovely flat, a company car, and some fantastic scenery. Within half an hour's drive from our home you could either be on the Pacific coast or inland in the mountains where you could go skiing.

But both Sandra and I were missing England and our families. Going back to Newcastle was the ideal move, especially as I now had the chance to play in the same team as players like Keegan and Terry McDermott. It was better than I could ever have expected.

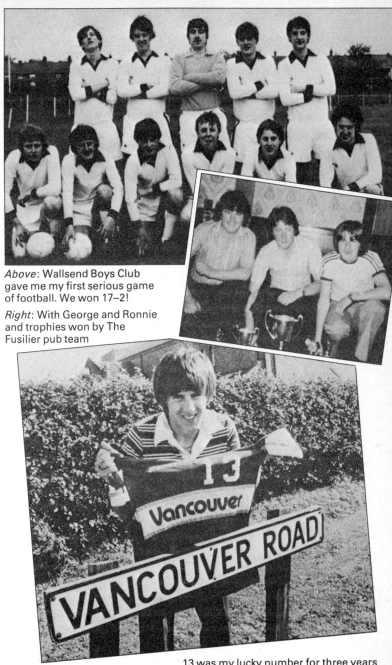

Above: Wallsend Boys Club gave me my first serious game of football. We won 17–2!

Right: With George and Ronnie and trophies won by The Fusilier pub team

13 was my lucky number for three years in Canada

Above: Playing for Vancouver. As you can see from the hair-style, I was still a big Rod Stewart fan

Right: Ray Wilkins – the best captain I've played for

Kevin Keegan was an inspiration to everyone at Newcastle

Alan Hansen has consistently been one of the best defenders in the game for the last ten years

Above: 'Jinky' Jimmy Smith – one of my first heroes at Newcastle

Right: Another late starter – Chris Waddle made his name with some sparkling displays for Newcastle

My wife Sandra shares my big day as I sign for Liverpool

Right: A reminder to the opposition!

Beardsley, Barnes and Aldridge . . . the Liverpool strike force

Roy Evans helps me off the pitch after a whack from Arsenal's Steve Williams left me limping in my first League game for Liverpool

The clubs agreed a fee of £150,000, and Sandra and I packed our bags and flew back to England. After landing at Heathrow we took the shuttle flight to Newcastle. As we were boarding there was a buzz of excitement among the other passengers and I overheard someone say that Kevin Keegan was on the same flight. Sure enough, there was the man himself.

He'd been one of my heroes. He'd won the first of his 63 England caps when I was 12 years old and had been one of football's biggest superstars ever since. I had a good excuse to go and talk to him, especially as we were going to be team-mates, but I was too shy.

When we landed in Newcastle, Sandra and I waited for everyone else to get off the plane first. We'd been travelling for 15 hours from Vancouver and were too tired to get involved in the pushing and shoving. When we climbed down the steps I saw Keegan was still standing on the tarmac. As we walked past he shot out a hand and introduced himself, apologising for not saying hello on the plane. 'I've only just realised who you are,' he said. 'Welcome to Newcastle. I'm delighted you're joining us. I'm sure you'll love it here.'

I was overwhelmed. Kevin must have thought I was a complete idiot as I just stood there with an inane grin on my face. But a combination of jet lag and astonishment at meeting one of my heroes had left me speechless! The following day the club sent a car to collect Sandra and me to take us to the ground where I met Arthur Cox. Within two hours we'd agreed terms and I was a Newcastle player.

They were the only club to come in for me but it couldn't have been better from my point of view. I used to watch Newcastle from the terraces and always wanted to play for them. I was back home near my family and back with another chance to prove myself in the Football League. At that stage money didn't matter. After the disappointment at being rejected by Manchester United it was important for me to get back into the English game and show what I could do. That experience at Old Trafford the previous winter had made me more determined to succeed than ever.

I thought I would have to wait for my chance at Newcastle but it came surprisingly quickly. I played my first game for the reserves in midweek against Leeds. We lost 2−1 but the following Saturday I was substitute for the first team's game at Barnsley. We were losing when I came on but Chris Waddle scored the equaliser to give us a 1–1 draw.

One week later I was in the team for the start of the game at home to Portsmouth. Arthur Cox didn't tell me I was playing until an hour before the kick-off but that left me plenty of time to worry about how I would play and how the fans would take to me.

I was lucky to get my first touch early on. The ball was thrown to me down the line. I could sense a defender rushing towards me from behind. As he committed himself to the challenge the ball was perfectly placed for me to flick it over his head and run into space. The crowd loved it, even though the defender had virtually invited me to do it.

From that moment I felt the crowd was on my side. It's funny how things work out. That touch gave me confidence and I settled down. But if I had messed that up and gone on to play a nightmare on my first game then everything could have turned out differently.

We beat Portsmouth 4–2 with Chris Waddle playing a blinder. He scored twice, including one from an incredible 25-yard shot, and was really buzzing and showing all his old tricks. But Arthur Cox substituted him. I was surprised, and Chris was devastated at the time. But Arthur explained that Chris hadn't been hungry enough for his hat-trick!

I think Chris realised that Arthur was right. It was a lesson for him and an introduction to Arthur's way of thinking for me. He was trying to instill the killer instinct and teach us to never ease up when you're ahead.

But I'd done quite well, and from then until the end of the season I missed only one game. It was the beginning of one of the most enjoyable periods of my career.

With so many characters at the club there were plenty of laughs. Arthur Cox had an image as a bit of a sergeant-major type with his short hair and strong ideas about discipline. The lads used to joke about the military style regime, and one morning we were training when we saw two figures dressed in army combat gear darting around behind the bushes. For a moment we were worried that it might be a terrorist attack then suddenly the 'commandos' revealed themselves. Keegan and McDermott had hired the uniforms for a laugh and worn them to training as part of the military joke.

Newcastle were promoted along with Sheffield Wednesday and Chelsea and scored 85 goals in the League that season. Most of them came from the forward line. Keegan scored 27, I scored 20 and Chris Waddle scored 18. We played some excellent football and the Newcastle fans responded to the team's success. Crowds were up again, with an average League home gate of 28,910, and only Liverpool and Manchester United had a higher average in the entire League. We also provided good business for the rest of the Second Division. When we played away the games were usually sold out.

Home games were chaos. The players made their own way to the ground and had to walk about 100 yards from the car park to the main entrance. But that walk could take up to half an hour by the time you'd forced your way through the crowds. Everybody knew that Kevin Keegan arrived at the ground early and it seemed that they all wanted to be there to greet him. He would be mobbed before every game and there were times when it looked as though he'd never make it to the changing rooms.

The man behind all the success was the manager, Arthur Cox. It was Arthur who had lured Kevin Keegan to the North-East and who encouraged his team to play such attacking football. Training was geared towards scoring goals, with plenty of shooting practice, and on match days he wanted the midfield to give the ball to either Keegan, Chris Waddle or myself, the three front men.

'If you don't play in your opponents' half, you won't score,' he used to say.

I've never met anyone as dedicated to their job as Arthur Cox. I live for the game but I'm nothing compared to him. Morning, noon and night all that concerned Arthur was football. He was always the first person in at the ground before training and he'd rarely leave before seven at night. If he went to see a game he probably wouldn't get home until two or three in the morning but he would still be the first one in the next day.

He never missed a day's training and was involved at every level in the club. When the reserves played away in midweek Arthur would be the first one on the coach, shouting at everyone else to hurry up. He was an immaculate time-keeper, and although he was strict on discipline he ruled through gaining the players' respect rather than by fear.

He wanted success but he also wanted his team to play good

47

attacking football. Keegan, Chris Waddle and I were encouraged to take people on and try shots from all angles. He was good for both Chris and myself.

We'd both broken into League football quite late. Chris had been working in a sausage factory before he joined Newcastle. Without being coached in the 'correct way' to play through youth teams and reserves, Chris had developed his own style, and that season he was the most exciting player in the Second Division. Defenders couldn't contain him and never knew what to do next. It was a pleasure to be in the same team as him.

To win promotion through playing stylish, attacking football was rewarding. Arthur Cox had been brave to adopt such tactics as most teams try to succeed in the lower divisions by either kicking their way to success or relying on the long ball game, where they continually pump the ball into the opponents' penalty area and hope to pressurise the defence into a mistake or seize on a lucky bounce.

I found it easy to settle in with my new club. I was back home for a start and I knew some of the lads like Kenny Wharton, Neil McDonald and John Anderson from the time I'd spent on trial there a few years earlier. I'd also played against Kenny Wharton when I was at school, and we had some lengthy and enjoyable chats and arguments about those games.

Playing alongside players like Keegan, Chris Waddle and Terry McDermott made it easy for me to settle into the team. The quality of their passing helps the player receiving the ball and the quality of their movement off the ball helps the player in possession.

I scored my first goal in our 2–0 away win at Cardiff, and in the next match I scored a hat-trick as we beat Manchester City 5–0 at St James's Park. It was still October and only our twelfth League game of the season but already some people were talking about that match as the crunch game between two sides chasing promotion. Newcastle were superb that day. We scored five and could have had ten. I know people often say that when they win well, but on that day we played as well as I've seen any team play.

We suffered the occasional setback that season, including a 3–1 defeat away to Carlisle, but we were always up near the top of the table. The supporters were magnificent and followed us all over the country, but there were times when we let them down badly. In particular there was one game at Cambridge towards the end of the season. They were bottom by a long way but still beat us 1–0.

One Newcastle fan was so upset at the result that he burst into the changing room after the game. He was a big lad, well over six feet tall and heavily built, and he looked quite menacing. He was trying to force his way in while Ian Liversidge, our physio, who was little over five feet tall, was trying to keep him out.

It's not often you get burly fans bursting into the changing rooms. He was obviously upset and some of the lads were scared he would turn nasty but it was all he could do to stop himself bursting into tears.

'Oh lads,' he cried, 'you've let us down. I've travelled all this way from Newcastle and you've lost!'

Newcastle took thousands of supporters to every away game. They were fantastic and travelled all over the country to cheer us on. I don't know how they did it. Some of them had jobs but I know many didn't. The area was suffering from high unemployment and those who had jobs probably weren't very well paid, but the supporters still managed to find the money or the means to get to the games somehow.

I know how important football is to Tyneside and I know how hard life can be if you're on the dole and how a good result for Newcastle can lift your spirits. I never take the supporters for granted and always go over to applaud them after the game. It's easy to do that when you've won but I still try to go over if we've lost as it's the only way to show our appreciation of what they've done.

We finally made sure of promotion with two games to go by gaining a draw away to Huddersfield. Unfortunately Kevin Keegan, the man who'd done so much to ensure our success, wasn't there to celebrate. He'd been concussed in the game against Derby County two days earlier and had been advised to stay behind in Newcastle to help his recovery.

On the way to that game Arthur Cox called me to the front of the coach and asked me if I would like to wear the number 7 shirt. I'd worn the number 8 all season, but 7 was Keegan's usual number. It was a great honour to be asked to fill his shoes, or wear his shirt at least, and I was flabbergasted to begin with.

'You deserve it for all you've done,' said Arthur. 'I'd be proud myself if you wore it.'

I've still got the shirt and it probably inspired me to play one of my best games for Newcastle. I scored one of our goals from 20 yards with David Mills getting the second. A 2–2 draw meant we were promoted to the First Division and the celebrations began. You couldn't move in our changing room for photographers and champagne. Arthur Cox was overcome with emotion and everyone was being interviewed.

St James's Park was packed to capacity for our final home game against Brighton the following Saturday. Keegan had said he would retire at the end of the season and this was to be his last League game so it was an emotional affair. Keegan was fit, and once again he was at the centre of the drama when he gave us the lead. Brighton's Gerry Ryan threatened to ruin the party by equalising before half-time, but in the second half we scored twice more. Chris Waddle headed the first and I scored the third with just a few minutes to go.

It was one of those goals that I'll never forget. Eric Young, the Brighton defender, had possession just outside his penalty area but he seemed to hesitate long enough for me to win the ball with a sliding tackle. The ball came away cleanly and as I stood I could see Joe Corrigan, the Brighton goalkeeper, come forward from the edge of his six-yard area. I looked up and chipped him, the ball just dipping under the cross-bar.

It was my twentieth goal of the season, a target I'd set myself on joining Newcastle, so it was a special moment for me. Furthermore Kevin Keegan's last League game for the club had ended on a high.

He decided to retire at the top and played his final game in his official farewell match against Liverpool a few days later. It was an emotional night which finished with Kevin being whisked away from the centre-circle by helicopter. As he climbed aboard I saw him hand his shirt to a policeman. Later that evening Kevin asked if I'd received the shirt. I hadn't. Kevin explained that he'd told the policeman to make sure he gave the shirt to me, but the officer had obviously decided it was a memento worth hanging on to himself.

I'm one of those players who attaches great sentiment and value to football shirts, and Kevin Keegan's would have taken pride of place in my collection. He'd been such an inspiration to me and everyone at Newcastle and had worked hard to help me improve my game. I made a number of approaches to the Northumbria police but the shirt still hasn't found its way to me.

Keegan had made such an impact on Newcastle that it was hard to imagine life without him. But we had plenty to look forward to, and Arthur Cox told me he was determined to sign a big name to replace Keegan. He said he was looking for someone whose style would fit in with Chris and myself. The man he wanted was Kenny Dalglish. What a signing that would have been, but Liverpool, understandably, were not interested in doing any kind of deal. Instead we started the next season without Keegan, without Dalglish and without Arthur Cox.

He fell out with the board over the length of his contract, and to everyone's surprise he left to join Derby County. The man they brought in to replace him was Jack Charlton.

7
JACK CHARLTON

When Jack Charlton was appointed as manager of Newcastle United I thought he was an inspired choice. He was Geordie through and through, he'd played in the England side that won the World Cup in 1966 so he was already established as a hero in the North-East, and he'd done well as a manager at Middlesbrough and Sheffield Wednesday.

He stepped into what should have been a marvellous job. Arthur Cox had revived football on Tyneside. The team that won promotion had captured the supporters' imagination with their attractive football and, although Kevin Keegan had retired, the groundwork had been laid to build one of the most exciting teams in the country. Jack Charlton had that chance but he wasted it.

I thought Jack would understand what the fans expected but it soon became obvious that his ideas about football were alien to what the players had been used to and what the supporters wanted to see. In his first training session he made it clear that the basis of our game would be the long ball. He told our defenders to get the ball forward as quickly as possible and he wanted a big centre-forward up front as a target man.

He spelt out how he saw my role. He wanted me to chase after balls that had been flicked on by the target man. That's never been my game. You need someone with pace, like Gary Lineker, to do a job like that effectively. I'm much better playing deeper and carrying the ball from midfield to attack.

It didn't matter to Jack that he was abandoning the system that had worked so well for us the previous season. He made it clear that he was the boss, and if he said it, we did it.

It became obvious we would need a target man to work the system successfully but Jack didn't buy just one, he bought two. Midway through the season Tony Cunningham arrived from Manchester City and a couple of weeks later he bought George Reilly from Watford.

Chris Waddle and I were pushed wide and used as wingers. That didn't suit me at all, and I found myself out of the game for periods, especially as our defenders' main priority was to knock the ball long for the target man. I was disappointed, especially as things had gone so well the previous season. I remember talking about it to Chris Waddle who was equally disenchanted with the new system. Like me, Chris felt his strength was beating players on the ground but now we were expected to chase after loose balls which had been hit forward in hope rather than to our feet.

Ironically we got off to a flying start under Jack Charlton. We beat Leicester, Sheffield Wednesday and Aston Villa in the first week and found ourselves top of the First Division. More than anything I think we caught the opposition by surprise. They'd expected us to play the same football we'd played the previous season under Arthur Cox and weren't prepared to be on the receiving end of a barrage of high balls into their penalty area.

But we knew it couldn't last, and sure enough we went to Arsenal the following week and lost 2–0. To be honest it could have been six as we were completely outplayed. The following week we were away to Manchester United and we lost 5–0. We'd played quite well until just before half-time when we gave away a stupid goal, and in the second half they murdered us.

Once we started to lose, the rumbles of discontent began in the changing room. The players blamed the new system for the poor results. It seemed terrible to abandon the style we'd used so successfully the previous year, especially as we were now in the First Division where opposing teams give you more opportunity to play than you find in the Second Division.

But Jack stuck to his guns and, as he was the manager, we had to go along with him. In the end it was Jack's pattern of play that led to Chris Waddle leaving the club. Chris had enjoyed a marvellous season in the promotion year and showed he could play in the First Division when given the chance. In our game against Queen's

Park Rangers at Loftus Road he was outstanding. He scored a hat-trick before half-time and set up a goal for Neil McDonald to give us a 4–0 lead. Rangers pulled back three goals to make it 4–3 in the second half but Kenny Wharton made it 5–3 to Newcastle with six minutes to go before Rangers rallied again and scored twice to level the match at 5–5.

It was one of the most exciting games of the season, and Chris Waddle's performance had caught the eye of the England manager Bobby Robson, who described it as world class. But after the game Jack Charlton was furious. He flew into a rage and pinned Kevin Carr, our goalkeeper, against the dressing room wall. I thought he was wrong to do that as Kevin wasn't at fault for the goals. Gary Bannister had scored Rangers' first while their second was one of the most unusual goals of the season. Peter Haddock tried to volley a ball clear from the corner of our penalty area, but his clearance hit Kenny Wharton in the face and spun round and looped back into the far corner. Kevin was helpless to stop it and it's one of the weirdest goals I've ever seen.

It had been a great game for the fans and we'd scored five goals away from home but Jack was in no mood to celebrate that or Chris Waddle's contribution to a memorable match.

Instead of building on our talents Jack went and bought his target men, Tony Cunningham and George Reilly, and pushed Chris wide. Chris's skill was being wasted and it was no surprise that he opted to join Tottenham rather than continue playing in a role he didn't enjoy. I was still under contract so there was no way I could leave. The fans were still being magnificent towards me and I just hoped things would get better.

I hadn't got off to the best of starts with Jack. When I signed for Newcastle, Arthur Cox told me that if we won promotion I would be given a pay rise the next year. Arthur had left but I thought the deal should stand so I went to see Jack Charlton. I'd done well the previous season and scored 20 goals so I felt I had a fair case. But Jack baffled me completely. His deal was so complicated that when I finally unravelled all the details it worked out he was offering me a pay cut!

One of the key components of Jack's pay package was appearance money. He offered his deal in glowing terms. 'If we play two games a week then you'll be doing very well,' he said. It wasn't until I got home that Sandra and I went through the small print and I realised there would be long periods when there were no games and I'd lose out. When we did our sums it worked out that Jack's deal would leave me almost £500 a year worse off – and I'd gone in to ask for a rise!

Jack and I had different attitudes to the game and those are summed up in a couple of incidents which amazed me at the time.

The first came in a home game against Luton. We were winning 1–0 and the match was into injury time when I received the ball around the half-way line and saw that Luton had pushed so many men forward that I only had one defender, Mal Donaghy, to beat. If I could get round Mal I would be through. Seeing the chance for a goal I tried to go past Donaghy but he put in a good tackle to win the ball and I lost possession. Within seconds the final whistle went, and just as I was shaking hands with the Luton players Jack Charlton came rushing onto the pitch and grabbed me by the arm.

He was in a terrible rage and started shouting at me: 'What do you think you're doing? You could have cost us the game!'

I didn't know what he was on about for a moment but he soon explained.

'You could have lost the ball to Donaghy,' he went on. 'And he could have run down the other end of the pitch to set up an equaliser.' I hoped it was some kind of joke but Jack was serious.

I've always believed in playing attacking football for the full 90 minutes. It's not in my nature to dribble to the corner flag to waste time – that's not what the crowd has paid to see and I know it infuriates most fans. Anyway, if I'd beaten Donaghy I would have been in a great position to make the score 2–0 to us.

I was disappointed with Jack's attitude and furious that he'd tried to humiliate me in public. If he wanted to make a point then he should have done so in private. As it was everyone inside St James's Park had seen him grab my arm and start shouting at me. The argument continued into the players' tunnel, where Glenn Roeder had to separate us, and again in the changing room.

It even spilled over outside the changing room long after the game when a couple of reporters asked me what happened. I saw Jack Charlton at the top of the stairs and said: 'You'd better ask Jack. He's the boss.'

Jack came rushing down the stairs and started shouting and swearing again. It certainly wasn't the kind of post-match press conference they'd expected from a manager whose team had just won.

The following week we played Watford at home. We were leading 2–1 with a minute or so to go when we were awarded a free-kick on the edge of their penalty area. I was on the ball and saw George Reilly make a run to the near post. I knocked in a quick free-kick and George headed it past Steve Sherwood in the Watford goal to make it 3–1. George was delighted as he'd scored against his old team, the fans loved it as their last memory of the game was a goal, and I thought everyone would be pleased.

But not Jack Charlton. When we returned to the dressing room he was obviously furious.

'What did you think you were doing?' he asked.

I didn't know what he meant and said as much.

'You could have cost us the game with that free-kick at the end,' he said. 'The goalkeeper could have caught the ball, he could have booted it down field to one of their forwards, he could have scored and it would have ended up a 2–2 draw.'

I couldn't believe I was hearing him correctly. I just didn't understand his methods or his reasoning and I could never agree with him. But Jack was adamant that he was right. And he warned me: 'Don't ever do that again while I'm the manager.'

That was the final straw for me. Jack hadn't even acknowledged the quick thinking that had brought the goal. He could have done that and then made his point that he thought we were being too adventurous. Jack often flew into rages but that was the worst. I've never seen a manager so angry after his team had scored!

But there were also some lighter moments with Jack, who's one of the game's great characters. He rarely took training, although when he did he threw in some good ideas and they were often enjoyable sessions. It was even more of a rarity for Jack to put on a track suit. He would come along to training wearing his best clothes. He'd turn up each morning in a flat cap, jacket, tie, trousers and moccasin shoes. If he wanted to make a point he would stride across the pitch and join in with whatever we were doing. Everyone else was wearing football boots and training kit but Jack was in his suit and shoes and they'd get covered in mud.

But even in his moccasins Jack was able to kick a ball as accurately, if not more accurately, than anyone wearing football boots. He'd offer a challenge to curl the ball to the far post from the edge of the area. He was astonishing. Still wearing his shoes he would get nine out of ten to either hit or go within inches of the post. Nobody else was as consistent. Then he'd be off, get into his car with mud all over his suit trousers and shoes and disappear for the rest of the day.

Jack loved to demonstrate things on the training pitch. One morning he wanted us to work on playing long balls from the back up to the forwards on the edge of the opposition penalty area. The idea was for the two forwards, Chris Waddle and myself, to switch and make cross runs with the ball played in for us to run onto. Jack, still wearing his suit and slip-on shoes, showed what he meant by pumping a couple of balls forward. They were placed to perfection. He then rolled a ball to Malcolm Brown, one of our defenders, and said: 'Right lad, now you do it,' and walked away.

Malcolm booted the ball but miskicked it. It hit Jack Charlton smack bang on the behind. Malcolm must have seen the steam come out of Jack's ears and he just turned and ran. He hadn't meant to do it but that was no help, and there followed the hilarious sight of Malcolm running off across the muddy training ground chased by Jack Charlton. To give Jack his due he laughed about that incident later.

Jack was a complete contrast to Arthur Cox who'd been completely immersed in the running of the club. Whereas Arthur was first to arrive and last to leave each day, Jack was hardly ever there. Often he'd pop in early on, make sure everything was fine, and then be off for the day.

We finished in 14th place in Division One that season but it wasn't the comfortable mid-table position it sounds – we were only three points clear of Norwich who were relegated. I was the club's leading scorer with 17 goals in the League, although eight of those were penalties. The supporters hadn't liked the way we had played and nor had the players. Jack didn't like anything fancy and players were scared to try something unusual or unexpected in case it didn't come off and Jack flew into one of his rages.

But by the start of the next season Jack had gone. His departure was as swift as it was unexpected. We played Sheffield United in a pre-season friendly at St James's Park. It wasn't a good game and the fans let their feelings be known by chanting 'Charlton out'. After the match Jack came into the dressing room and said: 'That's it. I've had enough. I've resigned.' As simple as that.

The new season was only a week or so away and we were left with the uncertainty of being without a manager. Four days later Willie McFaul was appointed as caretaker. He knew what the lads wanted and what the fans wanted. The long ball game was abandoned and we started to play football again.

Willie had been at the club for some time, first as a goalkeeper, then as one of the coaches. He knew my strengths and allowed me to play to them giving me more of a free role. But the momentum we'd built up during the promotion season under Arthur Cox had been lost. Instead of building on that success the club had let one of its best players, Chris Waddle, leave to join Spurs.

The club had showed ambition when it signed Kevin Keegan, and Arthur Cox had talked about signing Kenny Dalglish as a replacement when Keegan retired. But that deal never came off, and once Arthur left the ambition seemed to die. The club should have made a couple of big signings, even if it meant going into the red. The supporters would have continued coming in sufficient numbers to pay for the new players and we could have gone on to enjoy further success.

We heard that there were efforts to sign players but nothing came of it. Jack Charlton tried to sign Steve McMahon from Aston Villa but offered way below the asking price. Instead Liverpool paid the full amount and have reaped the rewards ever since. I think Steve would have come to Newcastle at the time, and, if he'd joined, then players like Chris Waddle and certainly myself would have stayed.

Jack is a one-off. To be a football manager you need to be a strong character and Jack is well qualified in that department. His decision to leave Newcastle was probably the best move for him as well. He quickly settled into a new job in charge of the Republic of Ireland international team and showed what a good manager he is with the right set up by taking them to the finals of the European Championships and the 1990 World Cup in Italy.

But things started to look up for me in Willie McFaul's first year in charge. We finished in mid-table, and once again I was the top scorer with 19 goals. I enjoyed a good season, impressed Bobby Robson, the England manager, and broke through to the full England team. By the end of the year I was off to Mexico for the World Cup finals.

8
ENGLAND

So often in football one player's bad luck is another player's good fortune. That's how I came to win my first cap for England. A friendly had been organised against Egypt towards the end of January 1986. But several players had to pull out because of club commitments – there were FA Cup replays during the same week – and others, including the Chelsea striker Kerry Dixon, withdrew because they were injured.

With so many regular names missing, the England manager, Bobby Robson, called up several uncapped players including Southampton's Danny Wallace and myself. I'd celebrated my 25th birthday the previous week and a call up to the England squad was the perfect present.

I'd always dreamed of playing for England but it was something that never looked a possibility in my time with Carlisle, Vancouver or Manchester United reserves. Chris Waddle had forced his way into the squad the previous year when he was still at Newcastle and that had acted as a great incentive. Ironically Chris was one of the players who'd withdrawn from the squad for the Egypt game because Tottenham were playing Notts County in an FA Cup replay.

The call had come out of the blue, and it shows how swiftly fortunes can change. Three weeks earlier I'd been feeling rock bottom after Newcastle went out of the FA Cup, losing 2–0 at home to Brighton in the third round.

If we had won that game and been forced to replay our fourth round game I too would have missed the Egypt match and may

59

never have had an opportunity to play for England. As it was, Newcastle had a free week and I was able to travel. It went some way to easing the disappointment of being out of the Cup.

As we had a free Saturday, Newcastle went out to Bermuda to play Nottingham Forest in a friendly and I had to fly back early on my own to meet the England squad for the first time at their hotel near Luton Airport. I was so excited that I couldn't concentrate on anything. My eyes passed over the words and pages of my book but I didn't take in anything.

I didn't know any of the other players and was so nervous about meeting them that I sat in my room for ages, too scared to venture out, until Kenny Sansom came to find me. He was my room-mate for that trip and it couldn't have worked out better. I'm quiet and shy while Kenny is lively and out-going and one of the great characters in the squad. He went out of his way to make me feel at ease and had all the new lads feeling at home as he went through his repertoire of jokes and impersonations.

I'll never forget how proud I felt in my first training session. We wore the full England kit, the shirts had the England crest and the track suit tops had ENGLAND written in large letters across the back. I was like a small boy with a Christmas present rather than a fully grown man going about his job.

I was named as one of the substitutes for the game in Cairo and came on when we were 3–0 up. Ironically, I replaced Gary Lineker in that match, and at the time I never thought that we would go on to form such a close partnership. I felt I'd played quite well and set up our fourth goal for Gordon Cowans.

There were plenty of people in England who'd said the Egypt trip was a waste of time, especially with so many first choice players missing. But I wasn't going to argue with the wisdom of fulfilling the fixture. It had given me the chance to achieve a dream by playing for my country and showing what I could do at international level.

A month later I was in the squad again. Gary Lineker and Mark Hateley were both injured and I started an international for the first time when we played Israel. After conceding a goal early on we came back to win 2–1, Bryan Robson scoring both our goals.

Injuries to other players meant I was in the squad for the next game, away to the Soviet Union the following month. I hadn't expected to start the match. Trevor Francis, John Barnes and

Kerry Dixon had withdrawn but the manager still had Tony Woodcock and Mark Hateley in the squad ahead of me. Then, once again, someone else's bad luck meant fortune smiled on me. First Tony Woodcock woke up with an infected foot that ruled him out of the game. Then, when Mark Hateley joined up with the squad after his game with Milan, we learned he too was injured.

That meant Bobby Robson was left with just two forwards, Gary Lineker and me. I know that he hadn't intended to play me. I believe he initially saw me as cover for Gary Lineker but circumstances left him with no alternative but to play us together with Chris Waddle playing wide as a third attacker.

Despite having a weakened team we played well and won 1–0. Even more pleasing from a personal view was the fact that I'd had a hand in the goal. Chris Waddle hit a long ball wide to the right wing for me to chase. A Soviet defender had the ball covered but seemed to hesitate long enough for me to surprise him with a sliding tackle and win the ball. I looked up and saw Chris still making his run towards the penalty area – he obviously had more confidence than most that I would win the ball – so I hit a pass which he took in his stride to thump a marvellous shot which rocketed past Dasayev, the Soviet keeper. It was a great goal and did wonders for my confidence.

I knew I'd only played in that game because all the other forwards had dropped out but I felt I'd done quite well. I knew that once the others were fit again I would probably be out of the team but I was hopeful that I'd done enough to impress the management.

I'd been lucky that my introduction to international football had been quite gentle.Neither Egypt nor Israel were the toughest opponents. They both had skilful players but we were the better team in both matches. I can imagine an international debut against a team like West Germany being far more demanding.

But I was learning all the time. When I was with the England squad I was training with some of the best footballers in the country. My game improved from watching and playing with them. International football had also given me my first real taste of man-to-man marking, which is far more common abroad than it is here. It took me a while to get used to but I enjoy playing against teams who adopt that style. For someone like me who likes to take on defenders it means that once I've beaten my man I'm likely to be clear.

Don Howe and Bobby Robson prepare for matches by practising against such systems. During training those squad members not in the team adopt the formation which we expect our opponents to play to give us a chance to get used to it and find ways to beat it.

Although the pace of international football is often much slower than we're used to in our domestic League matches, I've come off the pitch feeling absolutely drained whenever I've played for England. You have to concentrate for the full 90 minutes. In a League game you often get time to relax and have a rest when the ball is at the other end but in an international you always have to be aware of what your opponent is doing. Often it's as much a battle of wits as a contest of skill.

International players think so quickly you have to be alert and you're always involved whether you're taking your marker away to create space or going with a man to cut him off. At international level you know there won't be any weak links in the opposing team, everyone who's playing is the best in that position in their country, so every game will be tough.

The World Cup was only a few months away, and although I felt happy with my performances for England I knew there were a number of other, more experienced, players who were also hoping to go to Mexico. For England's next match, against Scotland at Wembley, Bobby Robson recalled Trevor Francis. Trevor played with a fractured cheekbone and I thought he did well. I was encouraged to be named as one of the substitutes, especially as Newcastle had played two nights earlier, losing 8–1 at West Ham. At least I was still in the manager's mind.

That West Ham game was one that I'll never forget. I don't think there are many players who can say they've enjoyed a match after they've lost 8–1 but I did that night. It was a wacky game and we went through three goalkeepers with me keeping goal for the last 20 minutes.

We'd played Chelsea on the Saturday where our goalkeeper Dave McKellar was struggling with a bad groin strain. We stayed in London until the West Ham game but by then Dave's groin was so sore he could hardly walk.

Our other goalkeeper, Martin Thomas, had dislocated his

shoulder earlier in the season and it was still causing him problems, especially as the pitches became harder at the end of the season. Martin wasn't really fit but at least he could run about and kick the ball so he played.

It was a disaster for him. After five minutes West Ham's Ray Stewart hit a fierce shot which Martin did well to parry, but as he made the save he put his shoulder out again. He was in agony but carried on until half-time. When he came into the changing room he was obviously in too much pain to continue.

The manager looked around for someone to take over. I volunteered but everyone laughed and instead Martin's jersey was handed to Chris Hedworth. He'd been in goal for about 20 minutes when he dislocated his shoulder. A long cross came over from the right and Alvin Martin, the West Ham defender, headed it towards the top corner. Chris dived to try to save it, but missed the ball and crashed into the post.

It was obvious that he would have to go off and, before anyone else could volunteer, I grabbed the goalkeeper's shirt. There were some unhappy looks from the Newcastle bench but there were no other volunteers.

We were already five goals down and, although I conceded three more, I made a couple of saves to keep the scores below double figures. I was particularly proud of one save. Alvin Martin hit a shot high towards the top corner and, as I dived to my left, I flicked the ball over the bar with my right hand.

Then George Parris broke through with only me to beat. I went towards him and moved as if to go down, he bought the dummy and rolled the ball the other way only to find me there to pick it up.

The West Ham crowd were great and started chanting 'England's number one' to me. Alvin Martin scored from a penalty to complete his hat-trick – each goal had been past a different keeper – and the two other goals came from crosses to the far post.

I loved my spell in goal and could have gone on all night. I even came out to punch away a few corners. The shirt was a bit large for someone as small as me and was particularly long in the sleeves where it kept flapping over my hands. I've always enjoyed going in goal in training but that was the first time I'd been in goal in a first-team match.

The next morning I had to report for the England game against Scotland. I'd stayed at Glenn Roeder's overnight and arranged for

Alvin Martin to give me a lift from there. As I sat in Glenn's living room waiting for Alvin to arrive I was dreading the next couple of hours in his car with him gloating about the score. Sure enough he went on and on about it, especially his hat-trick!

I've always got on well with Alvin, and although we didn't realise it then we would be room-mates during the World Cup later that summer. At the time, though, neither of us were sure of a place.

Before the Scotland game the entire squad was measured up for the official team suit for the trip to Mexico. They measured everyone, and in my heart I felt I was only being included to avoid embarrassment. I hoped to make the World Cup squad but my chances looked remote.

The first news I heard of the final 22 came in a phone call from a journalist who I knew was quite friendly with Bobby Robson.

'Congratulations,' he said. 'You're going to Mexico!'

Obviously I was delighted, and for the rest of the day our house was over-run by reporters from newspapers and radio, and television crews from Tyne-Tees and BBC Television's *Look North* programme. We've never made so many pots of tea in one day. It was overwhelming and I found myself repeating the same answers to the same questions, it was only the reporter who changed.

We lived in a quiet street in Hexham, and the neighbours had never seen anything like it. Without doubt it was the most hectic day I'd ever had with the press and by the evening I was so drained I fell asleep in front of the TV.

I'd never been away for longer than a ten-day tour before, now I would be away for seven weeks for the highlight of any footballer's career. I was so excited when I met up with the England squad and couldn't get over the number of free gifts each player received, just for being a member of the squad. One sports outfitter provided us with bags packed with leisure shirts, trousers, and blazers and another firm gave each player a personal stereo.

I was happy to be part of the squad and to enjoy the build-up to the competition. The FA had planned it perfectly. We stayed at a hotel in Colorado where the facilities were magnificent. We trained at the US Air Force Academy which seemed to have dozens of football pitches, tennis courts, gyms and swimming pools with everything in first class condition.

We got used to playing at altitude – an important part of our acclimatisation as Mexico City is nearly 8000 feet above sea level. The ball travels much faster through the air and I found that I soon ran out of puff on steady 50 or 100 yard runs.

The squad built up a tremendous team spirit and after a couple of warm-up games in Colorado we moved to Los Angeles to play the World Cup hosts Mexico in another friendly. Mark Hateley scored twice and I scored our third, my first goal for England, in a 3–0 win. I was also whacked on the cheek by a Mexican defender's elbow. It was an outrageous challenge and if I hadn't already lost most of my teeth I'm sure that tackle would have done the trick.

We also played the Canada team in Vancouver, which was a nostalgic trip for me. Bobby Robson knew some people from his days as manager of the then Vancouver Royals, and several of my old Whitecaps team-mates were in the Canadian side, including Bobby Lenarduzzi and Carl Valentine.

I didn't start the game but received a tremendous cheer from the local fans when I came on as substitute. It was nice to be remembered but I was more concerned about the man I replaced, Gary Lineker, who seemed to have broken his wrist.

Gary had established himself as our first choice striker and there was great relief among the whole squad when we learned that he'd escaped with a bad sprain and the arm wasn't broken.

We had to be up at five o'clock the next morning to fly to Monterrey where our first phase matches were due to be played. Not for the last time the England squad caused chaos. Just as we were about to take off we noticed a pile of suitcases on the runway. There was so much luggage with the England squad that the airline weren't able to get all the passengers' baggage on board and were about to take-off without it. One man complained and ended up on the runway next to his bags as the plane took to the air.

Midway through the scheduled time for the flight I noticed that we seemed to be flying between two mountains which were clearly visible through the windows on either side of the plane. It soon became clear we were coming in to land. The plane was so heavy with all the excess weight of our luggage that we'd almost run out of fuel and needed to stop to fill up again.

In Monterrey we were greeted by one of the biggest security operations I've ever seen. The airport was packed with police and soldiers, who were all carrying guns. I don't know what they were expecting but I made sure I was on my best behaviour. There were even two guards on our coach, both armed with rifles. The coach was escorted by a convoy of bikes and cars, all with sirens and flashing lights. There was no danger that anyone would miss our arrival, and we had the same convoy wherever we travelled.

I was delighted to be named as one of the substitutes for the first game against Portugal. It would have been nice to be in the team, but 12 months earlier I wasn't even in the squad so I wasn't going to complain – I just wanted to enjoy every moment.

I think we all expected to beat Portugal, whose players were rumoured to be on the verge of a strike. But it didn't work out that way and the lads were bitterly disappointed to lose 1–0. With ten minutes to go I was brought on with Steve Hodge in place of Chris Waddle and Bryan Robson but there wasn't enough time to get into the game, let alone make an impact. I came off the pitch with mixed feelings. I was delighted to have been brought on to play in the World Cup but obviously upset that we'd lost. We knew we had created most of the chances and should have won.

I don't know what Bobby Robson felt inside, but outwardly he was still confident that we would beat both Morocco and Poland to qualify for the second phase. Training remained good fun and spirits were still high. But the Morocco game turned into a disaster with Bryan Robson dislocating his shoulder and Ray Wilkins being sent off for throwing the ball away. And that was all before half-time.

Morocco should have taken advantage of the extra man and gone on to win, putting us out of the competition. But instead of attacking they seemed content to play in their own half and settle for a 0–0 draw.

The game against Poland has gone down as one of the great England performances of the 1980s. It was our last qualifying game and we knew we had to win to go through. A number of journalists had written us off, and with Wilkins banned and Robson injured there was all kinds of speculation about the shape the team would take. A couple of people told me that I would be playing but I didn't take it too seriously until the boss named his 11. I was one of four changes, with Peter Reid, Trevor Steven and Steve Hodge also coming into the team.

Ironically we could have been two goals down early on but a great save from Peter Shilton and a marvellous tackle from Terry

Butcher kept out the Poland attack. Then suddenly everything clicked and we started to play, cutting through the Polish defence almost with ease. Gary Lineker scored a hat-trick in a famous 3–0 victory. I've rarely enjoyed a game more, even though I was substituted with 15 minutes to go.

Bobby Robson deserved the success. He'd kept spirits and morale high even though results had gone against us and our performances had failed to reach expectations. The Poland game was the most important match any of us had played in. The boss eased the pressure by breaking with our normal routine and taking the players up into the mountains on the day before the match so we could relax with a barbecue and a game of cricket. It worked wonders.

Before the game I was obviously worried, especially as there was so much riding on the result, but again the boss put me at ease. 'Go and play your natural game,' he said. 'Don't worry about letting anyone down. Not everyone gets the chance to play in the World Cup so go and enjoy it.'

I kept my place for the second phase game against Paraguay in the Aztec Stadium in Mexico City. I felt as though it would be my day from the start. Gary Lineker put us ahead, touching home a cross from Steve Hodge, but I was pleased that, had Gary missed the ball, I was behind him in a position to score. Then in the second half I put us 2–0 up. Gary was off the pitch for treatment after being punched in the throat so I took up his position in the six-yard box for a corner. The ball was headed out but fell for Terry Butcher who hit a powerful right-foot shot which deserved a goal. The goalkeeper parried it but the ball dropped nicely for me to score into the empty net. It was one of the easiest goals of my career.

Gary came back to score our third goal, and I should have added a fourth. The Paraguay defence marked man-for-man without a sweeper and there was one moment in the second half when I found myself with just one defender to beat. I was running towards goal and pushed the ball round him. I guessed from previous experience that he would expect me to follow the ball and try to body-check me. Sure enough he moved over but I'd nipped round the other way and was clear. I saw the keeper come out but chipped the ball over the bar.

That match was my first experience of South American

defenders. I'd been warned about what to expect but it surpassed even that. There was plenty of spitting, punches in the back and taps on the ankles. I was quite lucky as they concentrated mainly on Gary. He'd obviously caught their attention with his hat-trick against Poland and they felt he was the man to stop. The foul that floored him – a blatant punch in the throat – was a disgrace, and we were astonished that the crime went unpunished, especially as Ray Wilkins had been sent off against Morocco for a far less serious offence.

I still think we should have beaten Argentina in the quarter-final, and I'm sure that if the game had gone on another ten minutes we would have done. They started off the better team but it was only Maradona's infamous hand-ball goal that tipped the balance in their favour. I was amazed that he got away with it.

I was on the half-way line and saw him jump with Peter Shilton for a ball that was obviously Peter's. The next moment the ball was rolling into the goal. I was convinced Maradona had punched it and Peter's reaction confirmed it as he chased after the referee pointing to his arm. But the referee had blown for the goal and turned and ran while the linesman, who had the best view, kept his flag down.

Maradona's second goal was special but not as brilliant as people have claimed. He spun away from Peter Reid and myself on the half-way line and then cut inside Terry Butcher. Normally Terry Fenwick would have come in for a tackle, but Terry had been booked earlier and any challenge which even looked unfair could have had him sent off so he held back enough for Maradona to go round him. By then Maradona was clear but he kept cool to go round Peter Shilton and slip the ball into the goal. He'd caught us cold immediately after the first goal.

By then the pressure was off and we started to play. In the first half the Argentine defenders had kept Gary Lineker and myself subdued. We were up against two markers and a sweeper so were having difficulty getting behind the defence. Trevor Steven and Steve Hodge had caused the problems in the Poland game by getting forward but they'd been held back against Argentina.

It was only when Chris Waddle and John Barnes came on and ran at the full-backs that we started to stretch Argentina. John Barnes played superbly, probably the best 15 minute spell he'd had for England. He set up one goal for Gary Lineker and so nearly created another. He dropped a cross under the cross-bar and it seemed all Gary had to do to score was let it hit him but somehow an Argentine defender dived towards his own goal and kept the ball out.

Had the game gone on another ten minutes we would have won. We'd outplayed them in the last 20 minutes and could see that they were worried. But it wasn't to be. Our World Cup campaign was over and I was back home in the North-East in time to see Argentina beat West Germany in the final on TV.

The trip had been a marvellous experience. I was lucky that my partnership with Gary Lineker developed so quickly. It came around by accident, and once we started playing together it seemed our games complemented each other. Gary is at his best when he plays forward, chasing chances in and around the penalty area. I feel I'm at my best playing deeper where I can drift around, join in with the midfield and push balls on the ground into his feet or behind the defence for Gary to run on to. He's so fast that he makes a lot of hopeful balls into chances. And because we play in different areas we never get in each other's way.

Gary makes my life easier because the opposition always put their best defenders on him. He attracts close marking because he's the recognised goal scorer, and after he joined Barcelona he became a household name throughout Europe while, with Liverpool banned from European competition, I'm an unknown.

With the defence concentrating on Gary it takes the pressure off me. In our European Championship qualifying game away to Yugoslavia, the defence were so worried about Gary they followed him everywhere. Gary didn't score during that match but worked hard running off the ball to create space for the rest of the team to exploit and we ran them ragged, winning 4–1.

When I consider the number of talented players who never won an England cap I can't help thinking how lucky I have been. I was fortunate to strike up such a good understanding with Gary Lineker and to come into the reckoning at a time when the England team once again became one of the major forces in world football.

9
FAREWELL TO TYNESIDE

I'd enjoyed my taste of international success and was hungry for more but Newcastle didn't seem to share my appetite. In the 1986–87 season we slipped towards the foot of the First Division and were everybody's odds-on favourites for relegation. We won only two of our first 15 games and were still bottom of the table at the end of March before a late revival lifted us to safety. We beat Southampton, Leicester, Norwich, Arsenal and Manchester United in a run of five wins in six games.

I picked up an injury in the game against Manchester United, and although I didn't realise it at the time that was to be my last game for Newcastle.

I was ruled out for the rest of the season and by the time the new season started I had joined Liverpool for a fee of nearly £2 million.

I didn't really want to leave Newcastle. I was a local lad and they had always been my team. I was disappointed at the way things had worked out over the last few seasons but I desperately wanted to bring success to St James's Park. However, in the end, Newcastle made it clear that they wanted me to leave.

I still had another 12 months of my contract to run and I was happy to honour it. There had been talk in the newspapers about various clubs like Tottenham, Manchester United and even Real Madrid wanting to sign me but I never heard anything definite and thought nothing more about it.

Then I heard that Liverpool had made an offer. They had just sold Ian Rush to Juventus for £3.2 million and wanted to spend more than half of that on me. Newcastle called me to tell me they'd received the offer. Willie McFaul said that, unless I agreed to sign a new three-year contract with Newcastle, the club wanted me to go.

I was left in a difficult position. I'd intended to see out my contract at Newcastle and review my position then. Instead the club wanted me to commit myself for another three years or leave. I would have been happy to stay if the club had been ambitious and was intending to strengthen the team but there was no indication that Willie McFaul had any plans in that direction.

Furthermore, Willie had talked about the three-year contract he wanted me to sign but he never showed me the contract and never talked in concrete terms about it. It was obvious to me that the club wanted to cash in by selling me for nearly £2 million while they could get it rather than wait until my contract ran out 12 months later when any fee would be fixed by an independent tribunal and be considerably smaller.

I was upset and angry at Newcastle's attitude. I'd given my all for the club over the previous four years and hadn't expected to be treated like that. Willie McFaul was trying to make me out to be the villain who wanted to get away, while the club made no effort to keep me. Stories that I was already earning £2000 a week started appearing in the newspapers. I knew that was rubbish and so did the club but they seemed to be encouraging people to discredit me.

Before long I even started getting a few letters from people calling me a traitor and accusing me of deserting the club. That was upsetting as it wasn't true. I loved Newcastle and wanted success there as much as the most ardent fan. I felt the club was letting me down.

When things started to move, Willie McFaul went on holiday. The club wouldn't let me speak to Liverpool until he returned and there was no-one who could give me details of the three-year contract the club were apparently willing to offer.

I wanted to get the whole affair sorted out with details of the contract Newcastle had mentioned or the chance to speak to Liverpool, but Willie refused to speak to me, saying he didn't like doing business on the phone. A couple of days later I discovered that Newcastle had signed Glyn Hodges from Wimbledon. Willie was still on holiday and had handled the deal by telephone. I felt even angrier. It seemed a deliberate snub. If he could speak to

Glyn, why not to me? I was even more convinced that they wanted me out.

Eventually I was given permission to meet Kenny Dalglish, the Liverpool manager, at what was supposed to be a secret rendez-vous, a small hotel in Wigan. It had only six bedrooms and Kenny had booked one where we could talk in private along with the Liverpool chairman, John Smith, and Chief Executive, Peter Robinson. Kenny was convinced that no-one would find us, but somehow the news leaked out and a couple of newspaper reporters and photographers arrived.

As soon as he realised the press were onto us, Kenny made arrangements to move to another hotel. I was kept hidden with Sandra while Kenny gave the press the slip, and within half an hour we were off to Southport to continue our talks.

Kenny had brought along his wife, Marina, who told Sandra about life in Liverpool. I appreciated a touch like that. Too often the talk excludes a player's family but this was a big move for both of us and it was important to me that Sandra would feel happy at whichever club I moved to.

I'd probably decided to sign for Liverpool even before I met Kenny Dalglish. Newcastle had made it clear they wanted me to go and no other club had come in with a firm offer. But once I met the Liverpool management I was even more impressed by what they were saying.

The club were positive and ambitious. They'd had a disappointing season by their standards. The team had finished second in the League and were runners-up in the Littlewoods Cup. By anyone else's standards that would have been a marvellous year's work, but for Liverpool it was disappointing. The club were used to success – the previous year they'd won the double.

Some critics had seized on this and were suggesting that Liverpool were on the decline. Not only had they gone 12 months without a trophy but they'd also lost Ian Rush, whose goals had been so important in their success and who many people believed was irreplaceable.

Kenny Dalglish was more realistic and I was convinced he knew what he was doing. He wanted to sign good players and build a great team. A few weeks earlier Liverpool had bought John Barnes from Watford and I fancied the idea of playing alongside him. I knew from playing with him for England that he was one of the most skilful players in the country. The club had also signed John Aldridge from Oxford and I knew he was a reliable goal-scorer. They'd received a lot of money for Ian Rush but were prepared to spend it in order to achieve success.

The talks went so smoothly that we agreed terms within an hour. I felt sure it was a good move but I still had a few things to sort out with Newcastle.

When I had signed my last contract with Newcastle it included a clause that I would receive a loyalty payment if I didn't ask for a transfer before the contract ran out. It was a common clause written into footballer's contracts and I knew of several players who had been transferred without asking to go who had received the money owed to them under those terms. I'd also heard of other players who'd been involved in expensive transfer deals who'd received a golden handshake. But Newcastle weren't offering me anything.

They had signed me for around £150,000 and now they wanted to sell me because they could make a handsome profit of more than £1.75 million. I thought I was entitled to a small share of that profit, especially as they were making it all off my back and more importantly because I was entitled to it under the terms of my contract.

Newcastle didn't see it that way and wanted to keep the money for themselves. They didn't offer a penny. So I decided to honour the terms of my contract which still had another year to run and start pre-season training with them as I was supposed to do. The lads were surprised to see me, and my presence seemed to be an embarrassment to the club. Normally pre-season training sessions were open to the press but this time Willie McFaul locked the gates to keep everyone out.

After training Willie sped through the gates and past the waiting pressmen but I stopped to explain my position. I'd bottled everything up for so long it was a relief to get it off my chest. I explained that I had never asked to leave the club and would be happy to stay until the end of my contract when I would be free to play for whoever wanted me, whether it was Newcastle or anyone else. And I explained that the ball was now in Newcastle's court as they seemed to be keen to sell me.

I turned up for training the next day and on the Saturday, when we went on a six mile run. I'd explained the situation to Kenny

Dalglish. He was very fair and said he would wait another year to sign me if need be.

It didn't come to that. On the Monday Willie McFaul called me in and said he would pay the loyalty bonus. It was a short conversation, and at the end I thanked him and said good-bye. I went straight to the training ground to collect my boots and that was the end of my career with Newcastle. I didn't even get a chance to say good-bye to the lads.

Some people said I was being greedy in asking for the payment but obviously I don't see it that way. It's not as if I were asking for a couple of hundred thousand pounds. The club were using me to make nearly £2 million. That was the value they put on my talents. They wanted me to go at their convenience so they could rake in the full amount so I thought it only fair that I should receive what the club owed me under the loyalty clause in my contract.

What I received was a small amount compared to the overall transfer fee. The whole episode had been a painful lesson, but I felt I was right to stick to my principles. I love Newcastle and desperately wanted to be part of a team which brought success to the town. My biggest regret in football is that I never played in a Wembley final with Newcastle. I would have given anything to walk out onto the Wembley pitch in a black and white striped shirt.

Unfortunately it was clear that others at the club didn't share my ambition. I was sad that my time with Newcastle should end in such bitter and unpleasant circumstances with bad feeling on both sides, but at least there was one consolation. I was joining one of the best teams in the world.

10
LIVERPOOL

I find it impossible to picture £1.9 million. That's how much Liverpool paid for me. I'm not sure how many suitcases they needed to get the money to Newcastle but I was flattered that they should consider I was worth risking that large an investment.

It broke the previous British record transfer by £400,000. That had been set nearly six years earlier, in October 1981, when Manchester United paid West Bromwich Albion £1.5 million for Bryan Robson. After that transfer fees in England had fallen, although around Europe players had been sold for more. Ian Rush had cost Juventus £3.2 million when he left Liverpool; Diego Maradona had cost around £4.5 million when he joined Naples from Barcelona in 1982; and AC Milan spent the equivalent of £5.5 million when they signed the Dutch international, Ruud Gullit. Within a few years Marseilles spent £4.5 million on Chris Waddle from Spurs, while in Italy Juventus paid £7.7 million to Fiorentina for the midfield player Roberto Baggio.

Football is run as a business these days and generates vast amounts of money but I can't see that anyone is worth £1 million let alone £1.9 million or £5 million. There's a good case for the introduction of a maximum transfer fee to stop the market getting out of hand. Once a club makes a tidy profit from selling a player they find it difficult to get a replacement at a fair price. If they make an offer for someone, that player's club will push up his value because they know the other club can afford to pay more. And so the spiral continues with ordinary players going for huge and unjustified fees. It would be better if clubs could use that money to improve the facilities for the supporters or even reduce admission prices to make the game more affordable for the ordinary fan.

But whatever my views on the transfer fee I was still going to be labelled the most expensive footballer in Britain. It was a title I was to hold for nearly twelve months until, ironically, another Newcastle player, Paul Gascoigne, was sold to Tottenham for £2 million. People say a huge transfer fee puts pressure on players, but I've never felt that. In fact it was a real boost to my confidence to think that judges as shrewd and respected as the Liverpool management thought I was worth that much.

I knew I was joining one of the best clubs in the country. I'd played at Anfield four times before but had never been on the winning side. My first game there was one of the most memorable matches of my career. It was Liverpool v Newcastle in the third round of the FA Cup on 6 January 1984. Everyone remembers that match as Kevin Keegan's return to his old club. After being a hero with Liverpool for so long Keegan was now returning to Anfield as a Newcastle player.

Such was the interest in the game it was played on a Friday evening and was shown live on television. Newcastle took around 12,000 supporters, an incredible number considering the game was on TV, and the atmosphere inside the ground was fantastic. Around that time it seemed that every supporter waved a flag or scarf, a fashion that declined over the following seasons, and the ground was a marvellous sight. Black and white at one end and a mass of red at the other.

On the coach journey to Anfield I noticed the number of houses painted in Liverpool's colours, and when we climbed down off the coach I was amazed at how friendly the fans were. They all wanted to cheer Keegan, who was obviously still a hero. That doesn't happen to many players when they return to their former clubs. More often the supporters who used to cheer them will be more inclined to jeer and hurl abuse when they come back with their new club.

We lost 4–0, but occasionally there are games you enjoy even though you've been beaten and that was one of them for me. The following season Newcastle were in the First Division and we were beaten 3–1 at Anfield but on my next visit it was a case of third time lucky. We drew 1–1 and I scored.

It was one of the best Newcastle performances of the season and we thoroughly deserved our point. I remember my goal vividly.

England v Poland in Monterrey, World Cup finals, June 1986

I score the second goal in England's 3–0 win against Paraguay in the 1986 World Cup in Mexico

My first encounter with a South American defender in the same game against Paraguay

A 3–0 win against Poland revived our World Cup hopes

Bobby Robson was quite relaxed before the World Cup quarter-final against Argentina in Mexico's Aztec stadium

In action against Argentina, Mexico City, June 1986

One of my proudest moments . . . captaining England against Israel, February 1988

Backed up by Steve Hodge and Mark Hateley during the 1987 Rous Cup match against Scotland

Markers stick close at international level – here I'm trying to get away from Scotland's Roy Aitken

John Bailey, the Newcastle full-back, booted a ball long and wide over the Liverpool defence towards our right wing where I was in space. It fell perfectly and I hit it on the volley past Bruce Grobbelaar. As luck would have it I was right in front of the Newcastle fans in the Anfield Road end and they seemed to enjoy that moment as much as I did. Steve Nicol scored an equaliser for Liverpool to deny us victory, but nevertheless it had been another excellent game.

Some teams are terrified of playing at Anfield. Most players have heard about the 'Welcome To Anfield' sign strategically placed above the players' tunnel on the way to the pitch. It's said it was put there to intimidate the away team – a timely reminder of what they're up against. But when I was at Newcastle we used to look forward to playing there. We knew we were expected to lose so if we got a result it was a bonus.

I'd always been impressed by Liverpool. Anfield was a magnificent arena with a fantastic atmosphere, especially at the Kop end. I'd never met with any nastiness there and the supporters enjoyed their football. I enjoyed games against Liverpool because you knew you would be allowed to play without fear of being kicked and battered.

Obviously they can get a bit physical in midfield if need be, but defenders like Mark Lawrenson, Alan Hansen and Gary Gillespie are skilful and don't go battering into strikers or try to chop down their opponents. When you play against Liverpool you expect to be closed down quickly and face a battle of wits against sharp thinking defenders, but you know nobody will go over the top in the tackle and try to hurt an opponent.

But although I'd enjoyed playing against Liverpool, when I joined I knew only four of the players. John Barnes, the other new boy, had been a regular in the England squad with me, and Barry Venison was a familiar face from his days with Sunderland when we played against each other in North-East derby games. Jim Beglin had been in Canada for a time when I was with Vancouver – Johnny Giles had brought him over from Shamrock Rovers – and I'd also met Bruce Grobbelaar the previous summer when I was on holiday in Portugal. He was staying in the same resort and we'd had quite a few chats around the pool.

Within hours of signing I was off for my first training session. Alan Hansen had shown me round Anfield before the club held a press conference to announce my arrival. As soon as the final photograph had been taken I was getting changed ready for the afternoon training session at Melwood.

The other lads had already set off in the club bus so I had a lift in Kenny Dalglish's car. As soon as we arrived the lads started taking the mickey and greeted me with plenty of comments about preferential treatment and travelling with the boss, but it was all light-hearted stuff and I couldn't get over how friendly everybody was. I'd been worried that some of the lads might resent the arrival of someone who cost so much money. I'd heard stories of players being frozen out when they arrived at their new club, but there was nothing like that at Liverpool.

There was obviously a good atmosphere at the club and a terrific team spirit among the players, even though there were so many fighting for the 11 first-team places. That first afternoon I paired off with John Barnes when we went running and he filled me in with details of who was who and how things worked. Liverpool had been back in pre-season training for five days and I immediately noticed a difference from what I'd been used to in the past.

I'd spent three days in pre-season training with Newcastle which was always hard. The coaches believed in plenty of six mile runs which were never popular with the players. One of the problems was that we never knew the route. The coaches worked it out beforehand and after seeing us off they'd dash round the course yelling instructions 'Left here' or 'Right after the next tree'. We were training around the banks of the River Tyne so the scenery was nice enough but I hated not knowing how much further I had to run. At least when you run laps round a field you can count down how many more you've got to run, but at Newcastle they enjoyed making it hard for the players.

After that Liverpool seemed easy. The furthest we ran in one go was about 1000 metres, and after some light running we went straight into a couple of eight-a-sides across the pitch. All the players were involved, not just the first-team squad, and the winners of one game played the winners of the other.

In my first three hours with Liverpool I saw more of the ball than I'd seen in three days with Newcastle. We still did our share of running but the Liverpool way was different. They concentrated on shorter distances and more repetitions. It was all geared towards what we'd need in a match and seemed more relevant than the long distance slogs I'd been used to.

Six mile runs are fine but footballers are never going to run non-stop for six miles during a game. You might cover six miles overall but you're more likely to run it in a series of ten or 50 yard bursts. That's what we train for at Liverpool.

The coaches like to include plenty of practice games and they'll introduce some innovative rules. For example, in a five-a-side, teams can only score if all their players are in their opponents' half. And if a team concedes a goal all their players have to be in their own half otherwise the goal counts double. Rules like that make the game more enjoyable and encourage players who would otherwise think about taking a casual breather to put in some running to avoid being slaughtered by the rest of the lads.

There aren't many players who enjoy pre-season training. The worst part is that you're in for both the morning and the afternoon. The players break for lunch for an hour and a half and stiffen up before the afternoon when it's hard to get going again. With Liverpool we at least knew there would be a game to look forward to.

I soon became used to the Liverpool way of doing things. Once the season was underway training would be hard at the beginning of the week and tail off towards match days. The typical week would start with a rest day on Sunday after the game on Saturday. We would probably be off Monday as well but if not we'd be in and ready to start training by half past ten.

We have to be in at Anfield by ten, get changed and go up to the training ground at Melwood by bus. All the lads get together, from apprentices to the first team, and have a good natter on the journey about what they did the previous night and so on. If we went straight to the training ground we'd be having those conversations in the changing room and during the early part of the session. Instead we've done our talking on the bus and are ready to give our full attention to training.

We start with a five minute walk which loosens any muscles that may have stiffened during the rest day and then go off on a three or four minute run. That doesn't sound much but you can normally cover about 1000 metres which is roughly the equivalent of one lap round the perimeter of the Melwood training ground.

That's followed by a series of exercises, several short runs and then into a game, probably seven or eight-a-side. We have the same teams every morning. I'm in what's known as the Staff side which also includes the coaches, Ronnie Moran and Roy Evans, John Barnes, Steve McMahon, Alan Hansen and the boss. The opposition, known as the yellows after the colour of their bibs, are usually led by Gary Gillespie and comprise the rest of the first-team squad.

We play two or three 20 minute sessions interspersed with a period of shuttle runs. The games are always enjoyable and the coaches introduce rule changes during the game for a touch of variety. We may play two touch or no ball above hip height or introduce the rule about teams only scoring when all their players are in their opponents' half.

Training normally follows a similar pattern for the early part of the week, but as the game approaches the workload eases. John Aldridge and I usually stay on for a while after training for some shooting practise. I go in goal, the boss supplies the crosses and John provides the shots.

They're good training sessions, hard but not the sort that leave you drained. Some clubs push their players so hard they're often exhausted by match day and too tired to give their best perform-ance. That's not the Liverpool way. Everything is geared towards the match, from the type of exercises we do to the amount of work we get through. The lighter training sessions on Thursdays and Fridays mean players have so much pent up energy they're raring to go by Saturday.

Ronnie Moran and Roy Evans have perfected a marvellous double act as the Liverpool coaches. They complement each other. It soon became clear that Ronnie took the role of the hard man and did the shouting and moaning at players when they were doing something wrong. A session from Ronnie could leave a player feeling low, and that's when Roy Evans would come along to pick them up again. He would explain that Ronnie was only doing his job and only wants the best for his players and Liverpool.

Roy has been brilliant for me. Both he and Ronnie understand their players. Roy knows I'm not the sort to shout my mouth off before a game but I still want to go out and play. Other players need someone to gee them up, and make them angry and annoyed to bring out the best in them but I prefer to motivate myself in my own quiet way.

They're both good players and still show their skill during our training matches.

Liverpool always train outdoors whatever the weather. Other clubs go inside when it's cold, wet or snowing but we stay out. The thinking is that we have to play in all weathers so we may as well train and get used to it. There are some mornings when it's wet, windy and freezing cold and you'll see the players hanging around in the shelter of the dressing room, showing no sign of moving until Ronnie Moran shouts at them to go out. We may not fancy it but there are plenty of people in other jobs who are out in all weathers and often for far less financial reward than we receive.

After training the players return to Anfield for a bath and some lunch and then have the afternoons to themselves. I believe that resting and relaxing is almost as important as training. I always try to have a couple of hours sleep in the afternoons late in the week during the build-up to match day. It's important to me that I feel fresh. Footballers put their bodies under a great deal of stress and strain and I need the rest to allow myself time to recover.

Everything is so well organised at Liverpool it makes it easy for new players to settle in. When we play away we usually travel the day before the game and stay in a hotel overnight. We travel thousands of miles over the course of a season and I usually take along a game like 'Question of Sport' or 'Trivial Pursuit' to help pass the time. I'm normally the question master and we've had some fiercely contested games in between the roadworks on the M6. Kevin MacDonald was voted the Brain of Sport, and whoever had him on their side usually won.

On match days each player has his own routine. Some are stranger than others. Bruce Grobbelaar goes into the dressing room at Anfield and tries to turn off the lights by chipping a ball against the switch on the wall. He does the same thing before every game. He stands six or seven yards from the switch and continually chips the ball against the wall until the light goes out. Once he's succeeded there's a big cheer from the rest of the lads, the light is switched on again and Bruce disappears to the toilet. Sometimes Bruce gets the light off quite quickly but on other occasions it takes him five or ten minutes and you can see some of the other players starting to get annoyed with the continual thud, thud, thud against the wall.

John Barnes likes to relax in a hot bath before a game. He'll soak for a quarter of an hour until about 40 minutes before the kick-off when he starts his stretching exercises. In the milder weather John goes out onto the pitch to warm up but when it's cold in the middle of winter he won't venture out until just before kick-off.

Steve Nicol likes to go through the quiz questions in the programme before the game. He goes into the corner with the boss – Steve asks the questions and the boss will normally know most of the answers.

Some players are very tense before a game but my routine has hardly changed from the days when I played for the pub side. I have to be in the changing room an hour before kick-off even though it only takes me a few minutes to get changed so now I get stripped and dressed in stages. The one routine I stick to is to munch my way through a couple of packets of chocolate buttons while I'm getting changed. I've been told that chocolate gives you energy but I've got a sweet tooth anyway. About half an hour before kick-off I go through a few stretching exercises and then, when Ronnie or Roy shouts that there's only 15 minutes to go, I put on my shin pads. I don't put on my shirt until we're about to leave the dressing room.

A few of the lads like to go on to the pitch before the game to warm up and kick a few balls around, others like a massage, and some prefer to sit quietly and gather their thoughts or read through the programme.

Kenny Dalglish talks quietly and briefly to each player. He never puts anyone under pressure. Some managers go on about opposing players, saying how good they are and building them up to be world beaters. That only makes players worry. Kenny concentrates on how Liverpool play and lets the other teams do the worrying.

The coaches make the most noise as they try to gee us up. Roy Evans knows that I'm quiet so he larks around and stares into my face and shouts 'Come on you!'. Ronnie Moran goes through the details of who stands where for free-kicks and corners before the final 'Good luck' as the bell goes telling us it's time to get out onto the pitch. I'm always the last man out. It's one of my few superstitions.

At half-time some of the Liverpool lads rush in for a cup of tea but I don't bother with a drink. The dressing room is usually calm while the boss goes through some of the things he noticed during the first half. Some managers jot down their thoughts in a note-book but Kenny is able to remember everything and go through where he thinks we're going wrong or where he's spotted a weakness in the opposition. It rarely takes him more than five minutes to have his say, and, by the time we've freshened up, the bell rings calling us out for the second half.

Again after the match Kenny will go through what he felt we should have done and where we went wrong. Some teams leave the inquests until Monday morning but I feel it's better to talk things over while they're fresh in your mind. I know we did well in my first season but I was amazed at how relaxed everybody was.

I take a long time to get changed after a game. I like to sit and go through the game in my mind before having a bath or shower and getting dressed. At Newcastle we'd either listen to the results on *Sports Report* or watch them come in on the *Grandstand* video printer on television but we never have a radio or TV in the Liverpool dressing room. Ronnie Moran usually pops off to find the other results and shouts them out to the lads while they're in the bath.

The training methods, the team talks, the whole routine was new to me, but it was the Anfield way. The system had been successful for Liverpool in the past and would be successful beyond my wildest dreams in my first season with the club.

11
DIARY OF A SEASON
1987–88

I signed for Liverpool in the middle of July 1987. The players had already started pre-season training. John Barnes had arrived a few weeks before me and we could sense that the club felt they were on the verge of something special. The team hadn't won anything in the previous season when their near neighbours and close rivals Everton had won the League. That was incentive enough for the established Liverpool players to do well this time round. I'd never won anything as a professional but I was ambitious and hungry to succeed.

I decided to keep a match by match diary. When the season began we were, like most other players, full of hope that this would be our year. But way back in the middle of summer I had no idea it would turn out to be such a remarkable season.

TUESDAY, 23rd JULY

Bayern Munich 3 Liverpool 2 (Dieter Hoeness testimonial)

My first game for my new club. I'd only been with Liverpool for a few days and I was still getting used to my new team-mates. John Barnes and John Aldridge are also relative newcomers and we found it difficult to adjust.

The game had been arranged in secret to avoid English fans travelling abroad. English clubs are still banned from European competition after the Heysel disaster and the FA had blocked trips by Tottenham and Leeds, who both wanted to play friendlies abroad, but sanctioned Liverpool's match. It didn't seem a true test of English fans' behaviour if none of them knew the game was on.

Bayern had been back in training much longer than we had and it showed. They were sharper and played as a team. Lothar Matthaus gave them the lead after 31 minutes, Dieter Hoeness scored a second just before half-time, and Wegmann added a third after 70 minutes. That stung us into action and we began to play. John Aldridge scored our first and John Barnes made it 3–2. We finished strongly but our performance failed to impress the English journalists who'd travelled over. The game was described as 'flat and uninspiring' by Patrick Barclay in the *Independent*. 'Peter Beardsley . . . was the greatest disappointment,' he wrote.

I wore the number 7 shirt, Kenny Dalglish's former number. Kenny wasn't too unhappy about the result. He said the game was meant to iron out fitness problems and help the lads get to know each other. At Liverpool they believe players can learn far more from a tough friendly game than they can on the training pitch.

SATURDAY, 8th AUGUST

Football League 3 Rest of the World 0 (Football League centenary match at Wembley)

The match to kick-off the Football League's centenary season. I had to rush back from Liverpool's pre-season tour of Scandinavia where we'd played six or seven games in 17 days. I flew back from Oslo early on Friday morning to meet up with the League squad and had to hire a dinner suit from a shop in High Wycombe for the centenary dinner that evening.

There were some great players on the pitch and it was an honour to be included. Maradona disappointed though. He was paid a reported £100,000 to play but rarely contributed much to the action.

The League won 3–0 with two goals from Bryan Robson and one from Norman Whiteside. Unfortunately the game became a bit of a farce as the World team kept introducing substitutes and their team lost its pattern.

Michel Platini was the star and won the man of the match award, but it was Paul McGrath who impressed me. I've always liked Paul and was delighted that he showed he could play with the best in the world. There are times when I wish he was eligible for England, he's so comfortable on the ball.

SUNDAY, 9th AUGUST

Celtic 0 Liverpool 1 (Tommy Burns testimonial)

I'd driven back to Newcastle after the Wembley match and then on to Glasgow. The boss put me as one of the substitutes as I'd played the game on Saturday and I came on for the last 15 minutes.

We won 1–0 through a goal from Ronnie Whelan. Afterwards Ronnie Moran seemed pleased with the way things are looking. We did well on our tour of Scandinavia and with the new season just a few days away we feel we are on the verge of something good.

SATURDAY, 15th AUGUST

Arsenal 1 Liverpool 2 (Barclays League Division One)

The season was only two minutes old before I was on the receiving end of my first foul, a kick from David O'Leary. That was harmless. The next, a couple of minutes later, was much nastier. A ball was cleared from our penalty area and, as I chested it down, Steve Williams put his studs down my leg. I felt Steve had gone to get me deliberately. People were crowding round as I lay on the floor and that shows they felt it was a bad tackle. I got another knock in the same place later on and had to limp off before the end.

Earlier the new boys had combined for our first goal. I'd played a pass for John Barnes. He put over a great cross for John Aldridge to head past John Lukic. Paul Davis equalised for Arsenal but Steve Nicol scored our winner two minutes from time. Not many teams win away at Highbury. A marvellous start to the season in front of more than 54,000 spectators.

SUNDAY, 23rd AUGUST

Atletico Madrid 0 Liverpool 1 (friendly)

Anfield was closed for the start of the season – a sewer had collapsed under the Kop and the authorities said the ground was unsafe until the repairs were complete. So our first few home games were postponed. Instead we played another friendly to keep us match fit, winning away in Madrid. John Wark scored the only goal after coming on as substitute. Futre was making his debut for the Spaniards and looked dangerous. I enjoy playing against foreign teams and the management seemed pleased with our performance.

SATURDAY, 29th AUGUST

Coventry City 1 Liverpool 4 (Barclays League Division One)

Coventry won the FA Cup last season and many experts were predicting that they'd mount a challenge for the championship this time round. In the end we played well and won comfortably. The Liverpool fans had once again travelled in force. Denied the chance to see the new faces play at home they made the trip to the Midlands and took up more than a third of Highfield Road.

I scored my first League goal for Liverpool. Gary Gillespie started the move and saw me run across the Coventry defence. I got the wrong side of my marker Brian Kilcline and, as he stretched, I gave him a little nudge. The ball broke for me and I saw I had just the keeper, Steve Ogrizovic, to beat. I turned inside him and slipped a shot into the goal. What made it even better was that it was at the Liverpool end and I saw the crowd come alive to celebrate.

I was delighted to score so early for my new club. It took the pressure off, especially bearing in mind the size of my transfer fee. I was expecting the 'What a waste of money' chants from the opposition fans and knew that the press would start questioning my value if I didn't score or play well. The other goals came from John Aldridge with a penalty and Steve Nicol who scored twice.

Some of our football was breathtaking. I felt good and was really proud of one pass where I received a ball from defence and volleyed it 50 yards across the pitch where it fell beautifully for Craig Johnston. Those sort of passes are almost as satisfying as scoring.

SATURDAY, 5th SEPTEMBER

West Ham 1 Liverpool 1 (Barclays League Division One)

Our third League game and we still haven't played at home. We had enough chances to win and led through a penalty from John Aldridge. But Tony Cottee equalised after a poor back pass from Alan Hansen of all people. We were disappointed to drop the points but Ronnie Moran and Roy Evans are more than happy with our start to the season – they hadn't told us before but at the start of the season they would have settled for three draws from the first three games, so the two wins are seen as a bonus.

WEDNESDAY, 9th SEPTEMBER

West Germany 3 England 1 (friendly)

England's first game of the season. Steve Hodge went down with a stomach bug so my Liverpool team-mate John Barnes returned to the team. Littbarski put the Germans ahead after 23 minutes and they went further ahead after a dreadful mix up in our defence at a corner. Just before half-time we pulled one back through Gary Lineker. Peter Reid had won a tackle and passed to me. I saw Gary in space and he put his shot into the far corner. West Germany added a third in the second half to complete their victory and looked a good side.

At half-time Bobby Robson had brought on Mark Hateley. I thought I might be taken off, as normally a forward will replace another forward, but Bobby Robson asked me to push back into the right side of midfield. I was pleased that he thought I could do a job there.

We flew back to Luton after the game and drove back to Anfield in time for lunch the next day. The club likes players to report after internationals so they can see how you feel and check whether you've picked up any knocks.

SATURDAY, 12th SEPTEMBER

Liverpool 2 Oxford United 0 (Barclays League Division One)

A month after the start of the season we played our first game at Anfield. The atmosphere was fantastic with more than 42,000 packed inside the stadium and another 3000 were locked out. Liverpool take the team away to a hotel for the night before a home game to make sure we get a good rest. As we made our way to the ground I couldn't get over the number of people along the route. It seemed as if half of Liverpool were on their way to Anfield.

John Barnes was outstanding. He crossed the ball for John Aldridge to score the first and then scored himself from a magnificent curling free-kick. After the game the players take it in turns to go into the sponsors' lounge to chat to some of the guests and fans and have photographs taken with some of the trophies the club has won over the years.

TUESDAY, 15th SEPTEMBER

Liverpool 3 Charlton Athletic 2 (Barclays League Division One)

Charlton surprised us and were twice in the lead. Garth Crooks scored their first with a lovely 40-yard lob. We pulled back to 1–1 with a John Aldridge penalty but Charlton went ahead again, Colin Walsh scoring from a marvellous free-kick. Alan Hansen made it 2–2 with a diving header and then Steve McMahon scored the winner.

SUNDAY, 20th SEPTEMBER

Newcastle United 1 Liverpool 4 (Barclays League Division One)

My return to my former club came early in the season. The game was played on a Sunday and shown live on television. We travelled up on the Saturday afternoon, listening to the radio commentary of Everton beating Manchester United on the way. I went to the ground in the morning to help put out the kit and have a look around the stadium where I'd enjoyed so many marvellous games.

As always at the beginning of the season the pitch was in good condition and I couldn't wait for the game to start.

We arrived early, and when the team went out to look at the pitch Steve Nicol, Alan Hansen and the rest of the lads started playing to the crowd, pointing at me and shouting: 'Here he is. The traitor has returned.' The supporters took it in good heart. There were a few who wanted to give me some stick but I received a loud cheer from other sections of the crowd which made me feel better.

As we were about to kick-off I shook hands with Mirandhina, who's taken my place in the Newcastle team. He's taken a brave decision to leave South America and become the first Brazilian to play in the First Division. I couldn't help wondering how he would enjoy it once the cold winter winds started blowing off the North Sea!

It was strange playing against players I'd been used to playing with. For much of the game I was marked by Glenn Roeder who was my room-mate when I was at Newcastle. I'd been worried about losing our unbeaten record against my old club but Steve Nicol scored a hat-trick and John Aldridge got the other in a 4–1 win.

We are now unbeaten in six games, with five wins and one draw. We've scored 16 and conceded six and are lying in third place. QPR are top with 19 points, Spurs are second with 17 points and then come Liverpool with 16 points and two games in hand.

TUESDAY, 23rd SEPTEMBER

Blackburn Rovers 1 Liverpool 1 (Littlewoods Cup, second round, first leg)

We scored early in the first half through Steve Nicol but Blackburn from the Second Division fought back and equalised through a header from Scott Sellars. The management are happy with a 1–1 draw as the second leg at Anfield is still to come. But as always in cup ties the team from the lower division had nothing to lose and Blackburn caused us some anxious moments.

TUESDAY, 29th SEPTEMBER

Liverpool 4 Derby County 0 (Barclays League Division One)

Derby came with an extra defender and caused us problems for the first half hour. But we took the lead before half-time through a John Aldridge penalty and started to play in the second half kicking towards the Kop. I scored our second – my first League goal for Liverpool at Anfield – and John Aldridge scored twice more to complete his hat-trick.

Peter Shilton, the Derby goalkeeper, was magnificent and kept the score to four by pulling off some marvellous saves. He'd arrived at Anfield without his gloves – they'd forgotten to pack them with the Derby team's kit – and had to borrow a pair of Bruce Grobbelaar's. But even with borrowed gloves he was magnificent.

The Derby manager, Arthur Cox, was my mentor at Newcastle and I popped in to see him after the game. Despite his team's defeat he seemed genuinely pleased that I was doing well.

SATURDAY, 3rd OCTOBER

Liverpool 4 Portsmouth 0 (Barclays League Division One)

I scored the first to put us on the road to victory. Steve McMahon scored a great goal, running on to a through ball and chipping the keeper; John Aldridge scored from a penalty; and Ronnie Whelan made it four. Once again we'd played well. I'd expected Portsmouth to be more physical than they were but it was John Barnes who bore the brunt of the challenges. Portsmouth are the first team to put two men on him this season, but John worked hard and created spaces for the rest of us by taking his markers on dummy runs.

TUESDAY, 6th OCTOBER

Liverpool 1 Blackburn Rovers 0 (Littlewoods Cup, second round, second leg)

John Aldridge scored the only goal in the final minute after a cross from John Barnes. But we should have made sure of the game earlier on, wasting several chances. Blackburn put up a lot of resistance but never caused us any problems.

SATURDAY, 10th OCTOBER

Wimbledon v Liverpool (Barclays League Division One) postponed

The high winds and floods which had hit southern England during the week made Plough Lane unplayable, although the game wasn't called off until a couple of hours before the kick-off. We'd travelled down the night before when there was no problem. The staff went to the ground in the morning and the match was still on but when they got back to our hotel we heard it had been called off. We had something to eat and drove back to Liverpool listening to the other games on Radio 2.

WEDNESDAY, 14th OCTOBER

England 8 Turkey 0 (European Championship qualifier at Wembley)

John Barnes scored the first after a couple of minutes, Gary Lineker the second after ten minutes. We were playing well, and by half-time we were 4–0 up, John Barnes and Gary Lineker again the scorers. Bryan Robson made it five and I scored our sixth with a header after a magnificent cross from Glenn Hoddle – it was my first goal at Wembley. Turkey still tried to play football and had a couple of decent players in midfield but Gary Lineker scored his third and our seventh before Neil Webb completed the scoring. I don't think England have received the recognition we deserve after that performance. To beat any international team 8–0 is some achievement and we are looking favourites to qualify for the finals of the European Championships.

SATURDAY, 17th OCTOBER

Liverpool 4 QPR 0 (Barclays League Division One)

QPR came to Anfield as League leaders after a great start to the season. They felt they had a chance but on the day we beat them easily. John Barnes was invincible and scored twice, his second after a memorable run from inside our own half. Craig Johnston and John Aldridge with a penalty were the other scorers. The management were delighted. In the dressing room Kenny Dalglish seemed more pleased with that performance than any other so far. It is the fourth game in a row that we've scored four goals and means we've won eight of our nine League games and have taken over at the top of the League for the first time this season. We've scored 26 goals and conceded six in our nine games and the supporters are obviously enjoying the way we are playing. Anfield was full again with another couple of thousand fans locked out.

MONDAY, 19th OCTOBER

Dundee 0 Liverpool 4 (George McGeachie testimonial)

I'd travelled to Carlisle after Saturday's game and spent the night at Sandra's parents'. The team bus picked me up just outside town on the way up to Scotland. I'd been on the bus for ten minutes before Kenny Dalglish told me that Ray Houghton was at the back. I thought he was winding me up and laughed it off as another of his jokes. But he was serious. He'd signed Ray from Oxford for £825,000 and, typically, it was the first I knew about it.

Our hotel manager in Dundee had recorded the controversial Rangers v Celtic match where Chris Woods, Frank McAvennie and Terry Butcher were sent off so we settled down to watch that once we arrived.

We trained the next morning where the lads started messing Ray about, getting him to do all kinds of stupid exercises but he took it well. I enjoy playing in testimonials, they are a nice relief from League and Cup games and there are no pressures on players.

I think testimonials are good reward for players who've given long service to one club and missed out on the financial benefits from being transferred. Unfortunately there's no guarantee of a good return. The team could be on a bad run or it could be cold and miserable on the night of the match which would keep the crowd down. George must have been pleased with the attendance at his game – 17,000 when Dundee's average home gate is closer to 6000 – and he came and thanked us after the match.

SATURDAY, 24th OCTOBER

Luton Town 0 Liverpool 1 (Barclays League Division One)

Much has been made of Liverpool's dislike of artificial pitches, and in the previous season Luton had beaten them 4–1 in the League and knocked them out of the FA Cup at Kenilworth Road. They were telling the papers that they'd beat us again but in the end they struggled to find their form while we played well and won through the only goal by Gary Gillespie. I don't mind playing on plastic and grew used to it in North America. Luton have shown that you can play good football on artificial surfaces, but although I'm sure that more lower division sides will introduce plastic pitches as vital means of earning extra income I think they'll disappear from the First Division. I wouldn't be surprised to see Luton follow QPR and go back to grass one day.

Luton's ban on away fans meant Gary's goal was greeted by silence – an eerie feeling after the noise our supporters have been making all over the country during the season. I admire Luton for taking a stand in trying to get rid of hooliganism. They're probably losing money through smaller attendances but at least they've done something to prevent trouble.

At the end of the game I could hear and see odd pockets of Liverpool fans scattered around the ground. They must have either joined Luton's membership scheme or found a way in as a guest of a Luton supporter. They'd been quiet during the game but were obviously pleased that we'd won and were past caring about hiding their colours.

WEDNESDAY, 28th OCTOBER

Liverpool 0 Everton 1 (Littlewoods Cup, third round)

My first Merseyside derby and our first defeat of the season. Everton deserved to win. Gary Stevens scored the only goal, seven minutes from time, with a shot that took a deflection off Gary Gillespie. They should have scored more but wasted a number of chances. After the game Kenny Dalglish was disappointed at the way we played, especially as we are out of a Cup, but at Liverpool the main priority is the League and anything else is seen as a bonus.

SUNDAY, 1st NOVEMBER

Liverpool 2 Everton 0 (Barclays League Division One)

Our tenth win in 11 League games. The atmosphere was even better than it had been for the game on Wednesday. Steve McMahon scored first and I scored our second as we took revenge for our midweek defeat. I was pleased with my goal – a left-foot volley. John Barnes started the move with a back-heel to set Steve McMahon inside his full-back. Steve crossed and John Aldridge's shot was blocked but fell nicely for me to volley. It was one of those shots which either goes in or ends up in the back of the stand.

I'd been getting some criticism in the press of late and hoped that my goal would go some way towards answering the knockers. I'd expected to be a target at some point during the season. I'd cost so much money that it was inevitable that people would start to question whether I was really worth it. I'd stopped taking newspapers to avoid reading the more hurtful comments but there was no escape. Friends would phone and ask whether I'd seen various articles and read out the most critical! One headline called me 'Peter the Plonker!' and was written by someone who'd probably never seen me play.

The Liverpool supporters had generally been marvellous to me from the start, although there were a few who sat near Sandra who would have a go. They obviously didn't know who Sandra was and she had to bite her lip a couple of times to avoid getting into an argument.

Kenny Dalglish was supportive. He told me not to worry about the newspapers. If I wasn't doing my job then I wouldn't be in the team, he said, which was fair enough.

WEDNESDAY, 4th NOVEMBER

Wimbledon 1 Liverpool 1 (Barclays League Division One)

The atmosphere at Plough Lane wasn't as good as Anfield at the weekend but we played well again and should have won. We had enough chances but managed only one goal, Ray Houghton scoring after coming on as substitute. Wimbledon equalised late on but we were disappointed to come away with just the single point.

WEDNESDAY, 11th NOVEMBER

Yugoslavia 1 England 4 (European Championship qualifying match in Belgrade)

The game was considered so important that the First Division matches at the weekend were postponed to allow the England team to have six days together to prepare for the trip to Belgrade. It worked. Bobby Robson had no worries about players dropping out of his squad with injuries late on Saturday evening and we had the chance to work together in training for more than just a couple of sessions.

If we lost we knew we would struggle to make the European Championship finals but on the day the game was in danger of being called off as a blanket of fog fell on Belgrade. It lifted just before kick-off. Within minutes we were a goal up. Peter Shilton kicked the ball downfield and one of the Yugoslav defenders back-headed it towards his own goal. I gave chase and could see the sweeper Marko Elsner was in trouble as he hesitated and let the ball bounce. The goalkeeper was slow to come out so as the ball came down I slid in and just got the touch to steer it into the goal.

As we grew in confidence Yugoslavia panicked. The second goal came from another terrible mix up in their defence. The goalkeeper rolled the ball to Elsner who was still inside the penalty area. I was right on him and he had no alternative but to play it and give away an indirect free-kick. Ironically we'd been working on defending against free-kicks from this position in training. Bryan Robson rolled the ball to John Barnes who drove his shot hard and low to the far corner.

Bryan Robson scored the third with a volley, and Tony Adams made it 4–0 after 24 minutes. At half-time Bobby Robson had a grin from ear to ear. We fully deserved our win, and although Yugoslavia pulled one back near the end we proved we will be a threat in the finals in Germany.

SUNDAY, 15th NOVEMBER

Manchester United 1 Liverpool 1 (Barclays League Division One)

Having been rejected by Manchester United it was nice to go back to Old Trafford as a Liverpool player. John Aldridge put us ahead with a great header. Alan Hansen had done superbly to chip in a ball behind the United defence, and Steve McMahon crossed for John to score. Norman Whiteside equalised but again we felt we should have won. Craig Johnston was disappointed to miss near the end after he'd seized on a bad back pass. Our draw means Arsenal stay top.

SATURDAY, 21st NOVEMBER

Liverpool 0 Norwich City 0 (Barclays League Division One)

Our third successive draw. Another disappointing result against a Norwich team that was struggling at the bottom of the table. They'd been a useful side last season, but after a terrible start this time round they'd sacked their manager Ken Brown. Bryan Gunn, the Norwich goalkeeper, was in good form and Norwich had the chance to win the match near the end, only a magnificent save from Bruce Grobbelaar denying Kevin Drinkell. I was taken off after 65 minutes and watched the rest of the match from the bench. The boss said he wanted to try something different but once again the papers started questioning whether I'd been worth the money.

TUESDAY, 24th NOVEMBER

Liverpool 4 Watford 0 (Barclays League Division One)

A big night for John Barnes against his former team. He scored a cracking goal and played well. Watford probably know more about John's tricks than any other side but even they were powerless to contain him. Steve McMahon, Ray Houghton and John Aldridge scored the other goals.

Ironically being taken off on Saturday probably did me a bit of good and I felt really sharp.

SATURDAY, 28th NOVEMBER

Tottenham Hotspur 0 Liverpool 2 (Barclays League Division One)

Terry Venables had just taken over as manager at White Hart Lane and the Spurs fans were hoping that he could revive the club's fortunes. I had picked up a knock against Watford in midweek. I felt alright on the Friday and wanted to play but the boss decided to leave me out. 'Better to be safe and miss one match than risk it and miss six or seven,' he said. Sandra was disappointed. It was her birthday and she was hoping to come down to see the game and spend the evening in London.

Instead I went in to Anfield for treatment in the morning and watched the reserves in the afternoon. I heard over the radio that the first team coach had been held up in traffic and arrived late at White Hart Lane. I wondered if it would affect the performance. It didn't. They won 2–0 with goals from Steve McMahon and Craig Johnston after Tottenham's Steve Hodge was sent off early on.

SUNDAY, 6th DECEMBER

Liverpool 2 Chelsea 1 (Barclays League Division One)

Our 17th League game without defeat, but Chelsea caused us problems and took the lead midway through the first half with a penalty from Gordon Durie. We won thanks to two late goals. The winner, three minutes from time, was set up by John Barnes with a back-heel to release Ray Houghton down the wing. His cross was turned in by Steve McMahon to give us all three points. Earlier John Aldridge had scored with a penalty to put us level. We're now five points clear of Arsenal, who are second, and 11 clear of QPR who are third.

By now we're getting used to playing on Sundays. At first I found that Sunday matches threw my weekly routine. I couldn't get used to spending Saturday afternoons listening to the results from the other games when I should be playing. The week seems much longer while you wait for the game to come and then you're faced with a shorter week before the next match. I'm a traditionalist on this and must admit that I prefer to play on Saturdays.

SATURDAY, 12th DECEMBER

Southampton 2 Liverpool 2 (Barclays League Division One)

Another close shave. Steve Nicol saved our unbeaten record clearing off the line in the last minute. Earlier John Barnes scored two marvellous goals but Southampton pulled back to level the score with goals from Colin Clarke and Andy Townsend.

I enjoy playing at The Dell. It's one of those compact grounds that creates a great atmosphere when it's full. When Southampton pulled back the place was jumping.

SATURDAY, 19th DECEMBER

Liverpool 1 Sheffield Wednesday 0 (Barclays League Division One)

Wednesday came to defend and frustrated us for 77 minutes. They played Gary Megson as a sweeper in front of the back four and he cut out the service to John Aldridge and myself. I was taken off about 20 minutes from the end.

It looked as though we would drop two points until Gary Gillespie scored. The goal came after a miscued corner from John Barnes. Ray Houghton flicked the ball into the six yard area where Gary side-footed it past Martin Hodge for the winner.

SATURDAY, 26th DECEMBER

Oxford United 0 Liverpool 3 (Barclays League Division One)

We trained on Christmas morning, went home for our Christmas dinner and then set off for our hotel in Oxford in the afternoon. I spent Christmas night playing snooker with the lads. I'm used to having Christmas disrupted after nearly ten years as a footballer.

I was booked in a game at Oxford when I was playing for Newcastle and the crowd there have given me a lot of stick ever since then. I don't mind and find it gees me up. In the end I had the last laugh anyway as we won comfortably, 3–0. John Aldridge scored against his former club to put us 1–0 up at half-time, and in the second half John Barnes made it two and Steve McMahon hit a superb 30 yard shot for our third. It could have been more and I hit the post.

We are now half-way through the League season and still unbeaten after 20 games. We've won 15 and drawn five, scoring 47 goals and conceding 11. Some of the papers are already calling us champions but the coaches make sure we keep our feet on the ground. Ronnie Moran keeps saying we've won nothing yet.

They've seen teams before that have started well and finished the season with nothing.

MONDAY, 28th DECEMBER

Liverpool 4 Newcastle United 0 (Barclays League Division One)

I know we have to lose a game eventually but I hoped it wouldn't be against my old team. In the end we won comfortably. Steve McMahon scored after four minutes to set us on the way. Paul Gascoigne played well for Newcastle but the result was never in doubt. John Aldridge scored twice and Ray Houghton added the fourth to take our goals-for total past 50.

After the game Mirandhina came into the players' lounge and congratulated us on our performance. I am delighted with the way things are going. Not only are we winning, we're winning in style, scoring plenty of goals and entertaining the fans. Once again Anfield was full and we put on another good show.

When I signed for Liverpool I was sure I had made the right decision, and the way the season is progressing confirms it. On away trips I room with the other new boy, John Barnes, and we can't believe how well things are going. John has been worried that the fans might not take to him, especially as there had been some delay before he signed for Liverpool. But his form has been so good he's become an instant hero.

Two months ago the bookmakers were quoting odds of 100–1 for Liverpool to win the championship without losing a game. By today the odds are down to 10–1.

FRIDAY, 1st JANUARY

Liverpool 4 Coventry 0 (Barclays League Division One)

A great start to the New Year. I scored twice and it is the eighth time this season that we've scored four goals in a game. John Aldridge and Ray Houghton scored the others. My first goal was a simple tap in but the second was more pleasing. I received the ball about 40 yards from goal and as the other Liverpool players started to make runs the Coventry defence kept backing off. I saw a gap and tried a shot from 25 yards which flew in. It was at the Kop end and I had a great view of the fans behind the goal as they celebrated.

New Year's Day always seems to be lucky for me. I often manage to get a goal, and a few years ago I scored a hat-trick against Sunderland in the big North-East derby match.

Once again we spent New Year's Eve in a hotel. A few of the lads were asleep at midnight but I stayed up to see in the New Year. When the clock struck 12 nearly all the doors on our corridor opened and the lads who'd stayed up were wishing each other a Happy New Year. If we continue playing the way we finished the old year, there should be plenty to celebrate at the end of the season.

SATURDAY, 2nd JANUARY

Derby County v Liverpool (Barclays League Division One)
match postponed

We travelled down to Derby immediately after the Coventry game. But we woke up to a downpour which left the pitch waterlogged and the match was called off. The news was greeted with groans by the lads. We'd played so well against Coventry we felt we would win comfortably at Derby. But we've played three hard games in the last week and the postponement gives us the chance for a break before we start out in the FA Cup next week.

SATURDAY, 9th JANUARY

Stoke City 0 Liverpool 0 (FA Cup, third round)

Players love the FA Cup and every year you wonder whether it will be your turn to get to Wembley. But the hallowed turf seemed far removed from the boggy pitch at Stoke's Victoria Ground. Bruce Grobbelaar had gashed a leg in training and missed the match. It was his deputy, Mike Hooper, who kept us in the competition with a marvellous save in the final minutes. A Stoke defender pumped a long ball forward and their substitute Graham Shaw found himself clear with only Mike to beat. But Mike was so quick off his line he smothered the shot to keep us in the Cup.

TUESDAY, 12th JANUARY

Liverpool 1 Stoke City 0 (FA Cup, third round replay)

A wet and miserable night at Anfield with a cold wind blowing in off the Irish Sea. I scored the only goal of the game after eight minutes, although we should have had more after having all of the play. We heard the draw on Monday after training and know that we now face a trip to Aston Villa in the fourth round. We don't mind that. They are top of the Second Division and going well but Villa Park is a lovely ground. The big worry had been a trip to a small lower division club with a bad pitch where the game can often become a lottery.

SATURDAY, 16th JANUARY

Liverpool 2 Arsenal 0 (Barclays League Division One)

Back to the League. The experts were saying that Arsenal were the team to end our unbeaten run and challenge us for the title. In the end we won comfortably. John Aldridge scored the first goal just before half-time but the credit really goes to Steve McMahon. He chased a ball which looked to be going out for a throw in, kept it in play and then cut inside beating two defenders before passing across the goal. My shot was blocked but John was there to knock home the rebound.

I was pleased with my goal. I received the ball about 40 yards out and saw that I only had one man to beat. I pushed the ball through his legs and was in the clear. John Lukic, the Arsenal goalkeeper, came rushing out but I managed to deceive him by dummying to side-foot the ball, and, as he went down, I chipped it over him.

Apparently the game was seen by a world-wide television audience of around 250 million people.

SATURDAY, 23rd JANUARY

Charlton Athletic 0 Liverpool 2 (Barclays League Division One)

Once again some of the papers were predicting a Charlton victory even though they were bottom and we were top. Charlton may have been encouraged by their performance at Anfield earlier in the season where they caused us problems and were unlucky to lose. But they were unable to repeat that today. Mike Hooper made a couple of good saves early on but then we got on top. John Barnes weaved his way through the defence to set up the first goal for me and then he scored the second goal on the hour to make the game safe. The crowd of 28,095 wasn't quite the 250 million who'd seen our game the previous week but it was still Charlton's best gate of the season by some way.

We're now unbeaten in 24 games and 17 points ahead of Nottingham Forest who are in second place. People keep asking Kenny Dalglish how this Liverpool team compares with others from the past. Kenny refuses to be drawn. 'We're not going to be playing them so it doesn't make any difference,' he says.

It's impossible to compare teams from different eras. Kenny obviously enjoyed some great times in Liverpool sides with players like Graeme Souness, Ray Clemence, Emlyn Hughes and Ian Rush and it wouldn't be fair for him to knock his old team-mates or put his present players down by saying the old boys were better.

SUNDAY, 31st JANUARY

Aston Villa 0 Liverpool 2 (FA Cup, fourth round)

Two goals in the second half saw us through although once again injuries forced a number of changes to the team. Gary Ablett played his first full game of the season, Steve Nicol moved to the centre of defence and Nigel Spackman came into midfield. But with Jan Molby and Craig Johnston as substitutes it gives an indication of the strength of our squad.

John Barnes gave us the lead early in the second half. Ray Houghton crossed and John headed past Nigel Spink. Afterwards John said he was inspired by comments from his former boss at Watford, Graham Taylor, who'd taken over as Villa manager. Graham had claimed that John had no right foot. 'I remembered that,' said John. 'So when the cross came over I headed it in!'

I scored our second goal just before the end. Barry Venison sent John Aldridge free, he whipped in an early cross and I hit a left foot volley into the corner. It was one of my best goals of the season, my sixth in six games and the 100th of my career. Once again it was with my left foot. When I was younger I was very much a right footed player but I've worked hard to improve my left foot and I've probably scored 40 per cent of my goals with it. The chances seem to fall that way. It may be that defenders force me on to my weaker foot but it's almost as good as my right now. Only a handful of my 100 goals have been headers. I remember one for Carlisle, my first goal for the club in fact, one for Newcastle against Derby and one for England against Turkey.

The lads are pleased to be through to the fifth round. The following day at 12.30 I tuned into the *Jimmy Young Show* on Radio 2 to listen to the draw and nearly choked on my lunch when I heard that we would be away to Everton.

SATURDAY, 6th FEBRUARY

Liverpool 0 West Ham 0 (Barclays League Division One)

Only the second time we've been held to a draw at home this season. West Ham came to defend and put all 11 men behind the ball. We weren't able to break them down and the few chances we created went begging. John Barnes had a shot from eight yards which looked to be going in until it hit John Aldridge on the foot and went over the bar. I knew then it was going to be one of those days. West Ham nearly stole it in the last few minutes. Mark Ward hit a 25 yarder which just flew past the post. Forest won and narrowed our lead to 15 points.

SATURDAY, 13th FEBRUARY

Watford 1 Liverpool 4 (Barclays League Division One)

I went out to look at the pitch before the game and could see that the heavy rain had made it a mudbath. Watford is a lovely friendly club and some officials asked me to sign a few autographs on my way back to the changing rooms. I went along to the area reserved for handicapped kids and had such a good time chatting with them I was late getting back to the dressing room and had to rush to get my kit on. It didn't seem to affect my game and I felt really sharp. I scored twice and John Aldridge and John Barnes scored the others in a convincing 4–1 win.

It was John Barnes's first game at Watford since he left and he received a marvellous reception from the crowd. They cheered his goal as if he'd scored for them!

WEDNESDAY, 17th FEBRUARY

Israel 0 England 0 (friendly international in Tel Aviv)

One of the proudest moments of my career as I captain my country for the first time! We'd met up with the England squad at the hotel in Luton immediately after our game at Watford. I asked the boss if the Liverpool bus could drop me off on their way home. The rest of the lads were taking the mickey out of the preferential treatment, with Ronnie Moran and Roy Evans pretending to be hotel porters and taking my bags in for me.

We flew to Israel on Sunday and on the Monday Bryan Robson strained a muscle. He'd stayed on with myself and Peter Shilton for some extra shooting practice after training and pulled it then. It was still sore the next day but the boss named him in the team, with Steve McMahon standing by in case Bryan wasn't fit. But after a few minutes training Bryan felt his thigh and went off for attention. When we got back to our hotel later that morning we learned that he'd already gone back to England – Alex Ferguson, his boss at Manchester United, wanted him home immediately for treatment.

The boss had left Peter Shilton and Kenny Sansom out to give Chris Woods and Stuart Pearce a game so the team was without an automatic choice as captain. There was plenty of speculation among the lads but I never thought it would be me. My guess was either Everton's captain Dave Watson or Mark Wright of Derby.

We waited for the team meeting that evening, which was held immediately before our meal. The boss said: 'We seem to have a problem. We haven't got a captain.' Then he looked at me and said: 'Do you fancy the job?'

I was stunned and couldn't wait to phone Sandra to tell her the news. She laughed and thought I was messing about to begin with.

I had a terrible night's sleep hoping that I wouldn't get up with a stomach ache or anything that would make me miss the match. The lads were teasing me all day, urging me to ask for extra bonuses and calling me 'Skip' but it was all in good fun.

It felt strange to carry the plaque and lead the team out. When we left the changing room I could see the stadium was by no means full but there were plenty of photographers waiting at the end of the tunnel. I felt so proud that day, and after the game Norman Medhurst, one of the England physios, presented me with a pennant signed by all the players.

We drew 0–0, with Steve McMahon having a good game on his debut. On the flight home I had to perform another of the captain's jobs. It was Bobby Robson's birthday the next day so at midnight we presented him with a cake. We didn't have any candles so one of the cabin crew held out a torch and as the boss blew she turned it off. I had to make a speech and once again the lads caught me out. They'd promised to join in a chorus of 'Happy Birthday' but once I'd finished what I had to say and started singing they sat there, mouths shut, and let me continue on my own!

SUNDAY, 21st FEBRUARY

Everton 0 Liverpool 1 (FA Cup, fifth round)

The lads would have liked to play Everton in the final but it wasn't to be. When I first heard the draw had left us with a trip to Goodison I thought: 'Oh no! What a nightmare!' but as the game approached it didn't seem a problem. We went there full of confidence and won with the only goal 15 minutes from the end, Ray Houghton scoring with a header from a John Barnes cross. A few minutes earlier Bruce Grobbelaar had pulled off a spectacular save from a Neil Pointon header – it looked as though the ball had beaten him and was about to go in at the far post when Bruce threw himself across the goal to make the save.

But John Barnes caused the biggest shock of the day by shaving his head. The club had taken us away to a hotel before the game and, as usual, John and I shared a room. We were due to leave for the game at ten past one but while John went down for a pre-match meal I had a rest. I was lying on the bed, and just before one o'clock John came in and started looking for his razor. I thought it was unusual as he never shaves before a game. Then, without saying a word, he ran the razor across the top of his head. I thought 'What's going on? He's made a mistake here!' but John carried on and shaved off all of his hair. Then he just popped in the shower as if it was all part of his normal routine.

I couldn't believe what I'd just seen but when I got on the bus I didn't say a word. The lads were becoming impatient to get away when suddenly Barnesie appeared sporting his new hairstyle. The lads couldn't believe it either. A few minutes earlier he'd been with them with a normal haircut for the pre-match meal and now he jumped onto the coach looking like Marvin Hagler. He was quite casual about it. 'I wanted to frighten the Everton defenders,' he said, with a big grin all over his face.

SATURDAY, 27th FEBRUARY

Portsmouth 0 Liverpool 2 (Barclays League Division One)

Our 27th League game without defeat. We've won 21 and drawn six, scoring 65 goals and conceding 12. Portsmouth had a couple of chances early on but as the game progressed we took control. John Barnes gave us the lead in the second half. His shot took a deflection from Billy Gilbert's leg and looped over Alan Knight, the Portsmouth goalkeeper. The second goal was a beauty. I worked a move with Ray Houghton down the right wing, and when the cross came in John Barnes hit a first time volley into the corner.

TUESDAY, 1st MARCH

Osasuna 0 Liverpool 2 (Sammy Lee testimonial)

A welcome mid-season break in Spain with a testimonial for the former Liverpool player Sammy Lee who now plays for Osasuna. One of the highlights of the trip was a guided tour round one of the local breweries.

We'd hoped for a few days in the sun but we arrived in the middle of a snowstorm and the game was played on one of the coldest nights of the year. I was one of the substitutes, and at half-time John Barnes asked me to rub some Deep Heat into his hands to warm them up. By the end of the game he was so cold he had to ask me to undo his bootlaces. It took him so long to recover that by the time he got to the showers all the hot water had run out!

SATURDAY, 5th MARCH

QPR 0 Liverpool 1 (Barclays League Division One)

John Aldridge had strained a thigh muscle in Spain and was still unfit. We trained on the Rangers stadium plastic pitch on the Friday. On the whole it's not a popular surface with players but we won the match quite comfortably. Craig Johnston set up the only goal. He beat his man to go free down the right wing and hit a firm cross shot which Dave Seaman, the QPR goalkeeper, could only parry. John Barnes followed in to score.

Alex Watson, whose brother Dave plays for Everton, made his debut for us at centre-half and was one of the day's successes. Rangers kept pumping high balls forward which were easy for Alex to win and he grew in confidence as the match went on. We should have increased our lead but I missed a good chance and Rangers put us under pressure near the end. Their supporters felt they should have had a penalty and started chucking coins at Bruce Grobbelaar. Bruce copes well and never lets anything like that unsettle him. He's more likely to pick up the coins and go to put them in his pocket. The crowd will laugh, it takes the heat out of the situation and they stop throwing things. I'm sure these people cannot realise how dangerous it is to throw a coin. The edges are really sharp and could blind someone.

SUNDAY, 13th MARCH

Manchester City 0 Liverpool 4 (FA Cup, sixth round)

I've never reached the sixth round of the FA Cup before. The pressure was on us as Manchester City are in the Second Division and had nothing to lose. I always enjoy playing at Maine Road and once again it was a good game. Ray Houghton put us ahead with a cracking goal. John Barnes broke down the left wing, got the ball to the by-line and whipped in a cross to the near post. Ray was in mid-air when he hit a side-foot volley which flashed past Mike Stowell, the City goalkeeper.

In the second half we started to play some great stuff. We went further ahead. Craig Johnston was brought down and, with John Aldridge, our regular penalty taker, injured, I stepped up to score.

saw Paul Gascoigne develop from a schoolboy at Newcastle into one of the most exciting players in the country

My first goal for Liverpool, away to Coventry

Holding off a close challenge from my Liverpool team-mate Ronnie Whelan in England's 1988 European Championship game against the Republic of Ireland

I thought we were unlucky to lose to Holland

Gary Lineker's goal against the Republic of Ireland sent us on our way in the 1990 World Cup

A moment of relaxation in Italy

To go out to West Germany on penalties was heartbreaking

Our semi-final against West Germany was one of the best matches of the competition

The play-off for third place against Italy was an enjoyable game with some great football

Craig broke through again to score the third goal. I was pleased with the fourth goal. I played a one–two with John Barnes and knocked a ball into his path for him to score. I think it's important to play passes which make it easy for the man receiving the ball and I was delighted with that pass to John.

Although we won 4–0 I was impressed with Manchester City. They have some good young players and I'm sure they'll be a force to be reckoned with before long.

WEDNESDAY, 16th MARCH

Derby County 1 Liverpool 1 (Barclays League Division One)

Craig Johnston put us ahead early in the second half but Derby equalised five minutes from time.

A draw means we're now unbeaten in our first 29 games in the League, equalling the record set by Leeds United in the 1973–74 season. We've won 22 and drawn seven, while Leeds won 19 and drew 10. We've also scored more goals, 67 compared to Leeds' total of 51, and conceded fewer, 13 compared to 16. The boss congratulated us after the game. 'You've done well lads,' he said. 'It's a fantastic achievement.'

People keep making comparisons between us and Leeds but I'm not sure who would have won. I was too young to appreciate that Leeds team but people say they were dour and always played it tight. I'm pleased with the way we've played – we have always gone out to play entertaining, attacking football. Funnily enough, several members of that Leeds side had a strong influence on my early career in Vancouver. Johnny Giles, who was the Whitecaps manager, was with Leeds in their record-breaking days, although he missed most of their record-breaking season. But Peter Lorimer, Terry Yorath and David Harvey had all played, and I benefited from playing with such experienced professionals.

SUNDAY, 20th MARCH

Everton 1 Liverpool 0 (Barclays League Division One)

Like Leeds Utd in 1973–74 we lost our first game in the 30th match of the season. Leeds had lost 3–2 at Stoke after being 2–0 up. Our record came to an end closer to home, just down the road at Goodison Park. Wayne Clarke scored Everton's goal after 15 minutes. It followed a corner which we failed to clear and he drove it in.

We missed John Aldridge. Without him there was no-one in the Everton penalty area to finish the chances we created. We were disappointed to lose and I think there were plenty of people hoping we would break the Leeds record. But the boss was quick to lift us. 'Don't worry about it,' he said. 'We've had a brilliant start to the season and no-one can take that away from us.'

WEDNESDAY 23rd MARCH

England 2 Holland 2 (friendly at Wembley)

Bryan Robson was back so I lost my job as skipper! More than 70,000 filed into Wembley. One of the main attractions was Holland's Ruud Gullit, the most expensive footballer in the world. Afterwards we learned that he was far from fit after a bout of sinusitis and was taking antibiotics. Gary Lineker gave us the lead but Gullit inspired Holland to score twice. First Tony Adams put through his own goal under pressure from Gullit and then Bosman scored with a spectacular diving header. Tony Adams equalised, but by then I was off the pitch after getting a knock.

It was my own fault. I was getting frustrated as for a little while the Dutch had us chasing shadows. Our defence wasn't pushing the midfield up and they weren't pushing up to support us. In my frustration I made a stupid tackle, gave away a free-kick and got a whack on the knee. It wasn't the knee that was so bad – I felt physically sick. I carried on for a while but felt so bad I had to lie down. Fred Street, the England physio, decided that if I felt sick I'd better come off as there was obviously something wrong with me.

The Dutch played some lovely football and showed they will be a force to be reckoned with in the European Championships in Germany.

SATURDAY, 26th MARCH

Liverpool 2 Wimbledon 1 (Barclays League Division One)

Wimbledon were the last team to beat Liverpool at Anfield and this season they've also won their way through to the FA Cup semi-finals. I'd recovered from my knock in midweek, and although the knee was sore I felt fit enough to play. Bobby Gould, the Wimbledon manager, was funny after the game. He came into our dressing room and commented on the speed with which players seemed to get over their injuries at Anfield, but the competition for places is so keen players want to get back as quickly as possible.

John Aldridge scored our first and John Barnes added a second. With three minutes to go, Kenny Dalglish came on as substitute for his first League appearance of the season. The lads were later to joke that he changed the game. Within seconds of his arrival Wimbledon scored through Eric Young! That's the first time I've played with Kenny in a League game and although he was only on for a few minutes we had time to combine for one lovely move.

SATURDAY, 2nd APRIL

Nottingham Forest 2 Liverpool 1 (Barclays League Division One)

The first of three important games against Forest in the space of ten days – next week we are due to play them in the semi-final of the FA Cup. I always sit next to Ray Houghton on the team coach with Kenny Dalglish normally in the seat just across the aisle. On the way to the ground from our hotel he leaned over for a quiet word and said he was leaving both Ray and myself out of today's game. 'I want to try something different,' he said. He must have seen how disappointed we looked as he added: 'Don't worry, you'll both play in the semi-final next week.'

The lads were even more surprised when he announced the team in the dressing room, and it was funny to see the shock on their faces. In the end I came on as substitute but we lost 2–1, only our second League defeat of the season. Alan Hansen headed an own goal for their first and Neil Webb scored Forest's second. In between goals Nigel Clough had a penalty saved by Bruce Grobbelaar. We fought back with a penalty from John Aldridge, and then Steve Sutton, the Forest goalkeeper, made a splendid save in the last minute to stop a shot from John Barnes.

MONDAY, 4th APRIL

Liverpool 3 Manchester United 3 (Barclays League Division One)

One of the best games of the season according to most of the papers. United have a good record at Anfield and haven't lost there since Boxing Day in 1979. They started well again today, taking the lead after three minutes through Bryan Robson. We stormed the United goal and drew level after half an hour, Ray Houghton setting up the chance for me to score.

Just before half-time we went ahead after I hit a cross to the far post and John Barnes headed it back for Gary Gillespie to score. The match looked safe when Steve McMahon hit a 20 yarder to make it 3–1 and then United's Colin Gibson was sent off. I thought Norman Whiteside was fortunate not to follow after a couple of heavy challenges on Steve McMahon and John Barnes.

But then the game swung United's way. Possibly we became complacent about playing against ten men, but first Bryan Robson's shot took a deflection from Gary Gillespie to make it 3–2 and then Gordon Strachan made it 3–3 after Peter Davenport lobbed the ball over our defence for him to run on to and beat Bruce Grobbelaar.

After the game, Alex Ferguson, the United manager, claimed that teams needed a miracle to get a result at Anfield because the officials were intimidated by the crowd. I can't agree. I played at Anfield as a Newcastle player and it's just like any other big ground, like Old Trafford for example, where there's massive support for the home team and an excellent atmosphere. It should inspire players and officials rather than intimidate them.

SATURDAY, 9th APRIL

Liverpool 2 Nottingham Forest 1 (FA Cup semi-final, at Hillsborough)

We learned some lessons from our defeat against Forest last week. John Barnes worked hard all game, and early on did well defensively to cover back and subdue Forest's winger Gary Crosby, who caused us so many problems seven days ago. John also set up our first goal.

He got behind his marker, Steve Chettle, and as he ran into the penalty area Chettle brought him down. This morning one of the papers carried a story about the Forest full-back, headlined 'I'll have Barnes on toast!' Steve Chettle probably didn't say that but Barnesie read the story and if he needed an incentive to do well that was it.

John Aldridge scored the penalty and then we went two up, following a familiar move down the left wing. Barnesie worked a one–two with me and then hit a cross first time for John Aldridge to volley in. Forest pulled one back, Nigel Clough scoring after a mix up in our defence but the result was never in doubt.

After the game Brian Clough was full of praise for Liverpool. He must have been heartbroken to see his team lose but he hid his disappointment and stood with his arm around me outside the changing rooms while he gave lengthy interviews. He's a marvellous manager and I like the way his Forest team play – good football with plenty of skilful players and no arguing with officials.

We heard that Wimbledon would be our opponents at Wembley. They had beaten Luton 2–1 in the other semi-final to complete a remarkable rise from non-League side to Cup finalists in 11 years.

WEDNESDAY, 13th APRIL

Liverpool 5 Nottingham Forest 0 (Barclays League Division One)

We started the game needing just five points from seven matches to make sure of the championship. Before the game Kenny Dalglish told us to go out and enjoy ourselves. We did. Ray Houghton scored the first, finishing a marvellous move involving Hansen and Barnes. John Aldridge scored the second, running on to a long pass from me.

At half-time Kenny told us to keep attacking. Other managers might have erred on the side of caution and preferred to protect the lead but Kenny reckoned the way we were playing we could have scored six. We didn't manage that many but came close. Gary Gillespie scored the third, I scored the fourth after Barnesie nutmegged Steve Chettle and pulled the ball back across the penalty area, and then John Aldridge scored the fifth after Nigel Spackman worked an opening on the left.

The match was shown on television the same evening and a number of people were saying it was the best team performance they could remember from an English club side.

SATURDAY, 16th APRIL

Mercantile Credit Centenary Festival (Wembley)

The League programme was scrapped for the weekend to make way for what was billed as one of the highlights of the League's centenary season. Originally all 92 clubs were to have taken part in a six-a-side tournament but that was eventually abandoned as impractical. Instead 16 teams – eight from the First Division, four from the Second and two each from the Third and Fourth – who'd had the best playing record over a period midway during the season, were invited to a knock-out competition over two days. It didn't capture the public's imagination and there were vast empty spaces around the stadium for the duration of the competition.

Liverpool were knocked out in the first round by Newcastle. We'd travelled down to London on the Friday night, and because our game was in the morning we had to be up for our pre-match meal at eight o'clock. The boss left me out as we were playing my old club and instead he played some of our reserves. We outplayed Newcastle but couldn't score. Then, with only a few minutes to go, John Barnes felt his groin and started to hobble off. I got on with 30 seconds to go but never touched the ball.

The game finished 0–0 and went to penalties. Steve McMahon took the first and missed, the keeper blocking the shot with his legs. Neil McDonald scored for Newcastle and they went through.

We were annoyed at suggestions that we hadn't taken it seriously and I thought we played as well in that 40 minutes as we played all season. But it was probably a blessing as if we'd got through to the final we'd have stayed down another day and probably been tired when we got back to Liverpool for training on the Monday.

Fourth Division Tranmere were the stars of the competition. They beat Wimbledon and reached the semi-finals before losing to Forest. In the final Forest beat Sheffield Wednesday on penalties.

It was a great chance for teams like Tranmere and Wolves to

play at Wembley but the competition should have been seeded. That way the organisers would have avoided games like Wigan v Sunderland at the start and there would have been the prospect of either some giant-killing, which always creates interest, or the big clubs with the big following getting through to the final stages. The timing of the competition was probably wrong, with clubs at a crucial point in the season, forced to interrupt their battle for promotion or against relegation.

WEDNESDAY, 20th APRIL

Norwich City 0 Liverpool 0 (Barclays League Division One)

We needed to win to become champions but came away with a 0–0 draw and several bruises. Every time I got the ball I seemed to get kicked. I should have scored early on but missed a couple of decent chances. In the end the draw was a good result as it meant we could win the championship in our next home game against Tottenham.

SATURDAY, 23rd APRIL

Liverpool 1 Tottenham 0 (Barclays League Division One)

The game that finally made the championship certain. I scored the only goal after 34 minutes but we never really hit our best form. It was disappointing but we've played well in 30 of our 35 games so far, so it's not a bad record, and at this stage of the season the result is more important than the performance.

I was pleased with my goal, especially as it was the goal that clinched the championship. Ray Houghton's pass found me in space on the right and as I cut into the Spurs penalty area I could see a gap at the far post and managed to thread the ball through for the goal.

It's my first medal as a professional and a moment to savour as we did a lap of honour after the match. The fans have been magnificent all season and once again they stayed on to give us a marvellous reception. My only disappointment was that John Barnes was injured and missed the game. He's been so influential throughout the season it seemed a terrible shame for him to miss the moment of glory.

It is Liverpool's 17th championship and their tenth in 16 seasons. We have won the championship with some memorable football and we all feel we can improve over the coming seasons.

The dressing room was chaos, packed with reporters and television crews. Most of the lads were drinking champagne but I sat quietly in the corner with my soft drinks – I never drink alcohol and have always been teetotal. Some people think it's strange but I've never liked beer or spirits.

I reflected on our success. The team contained some marvellous individual players but what was important was that they all worked for the team. People keep asking me about the secret of Liverpool's success but there isn't a secret. They pick good players and play simple football. There's also a flexibility about the team. The outfield players are encouraged to do what they think best. If, for example, Gary Gillespie sees an opening in attack then he pushes forward and someone else covers for him. If one of the midfield men pushes up then either John Barnes or I will drop back to cover if needed. All season we've been encouraged to try the unexpected and to do something different rather than play the predictable pass. There are times when we've had to be cautious but we've never been in trouble for trying to be adventurous.

Another reason for our success has been the quality of the squad. If a player is injured then there's probably someone just as good waiting to take his place. When Bruce Grobbelaar missed a few matches Mike Hooper took his place and played superbly. When Ronnie Whelan was injured Nigel Spackman came in and did a marvellous job. And there were games when we had players of the calibre of Jan Molby and Craig Johnston as substitutes.

Bill Shankly used to joke about the two best teams in England being Liverpool and Liverpool reserves. Looking at our second team there are many who would agree.

It is turning out to be an extraordinary season. In the evening I celebrated my first football medal at home with Sandra. We sat in front of the television and munched our way through some fish and chips from the local take-away. I didn't have long to enjoy the moment – Sunday morning I had to be up early to travel down to Luton and meet up with the England team.

WEDNESDAY, 27th APRIL

Hungary 0 England 0 (friendly in Budapest)

A first cap for Middlesbrough's central defender Gary Pallister, and Steve McMahon also played, a deserved reward for his consistency with Liverpool throughout the season. The game ended goal-less but Glenn Hoddle livened it up when he came on as substitute with some delightful passing.

SATURDAY, 30th APRIL

Chelsea 1 Liverpool 1 (Barclays League Division One)

We watched a preview of Craig Johnston's video for the Cup final record, the Anfield Rap, on the way down to London which put the lads in good heart. It's different for a football record at least! Once again the boss gave me a rest and named me as substitute.

I came on for John Aldridge after an hour, and a few minutes later Chelsea went ahead thanks to a Gordon Durie penalty. John Barnes equalised with a free-kick driven under the angle of the bar and the post, and I should have given us the lead, and the match, from a penalty three minutes from the end. The Chelsea keeper, Kevin Hitchcock, saved it to earn his side a much needed point in their fight to avoid relegation. Kenny Dalglish was quite good about it. 'You've been bribed,' he joked. 'You've been got at. How much did Chelsea pay you to miss?'

MONDAY, 2nd MAY

Liverpool 1 Southampton 1 (Barclays League Division One)

The League trophy presentation was carried out before the game with another lap of honour. To be honest it was such a great moment that the rest of the afternoon was inevitably going to be an anti-climax. Without intending to, the lads switched off before the match and relaxed too much. John Aldridge gave us the lead but Rodney Wallace volleyed a great equaliser for Southampton. We knew we didn't play well and with the benefit of hindsight perhaps it would have been better to hand out the trophies after the game.

SATURDAY, 7th MAY

Sheffield Wednesday 1 Liverpool 5 (Barclays League Division One)

The Cup final is only a week away and we warmed up with an emphatic win against Sheffield Wednesday at Hillsborough. We played some great stuff. Craig Johnston and I both scored twice, with John Barnes getting the other goal. We hit the post a couple of times so it could have been more.

MONDAY, 9th MAY

Liverpool 1 Luton Town 1 (Barclays League Division One)

Our final League game. The boss asked me if I'd appreciate a rest and also left out Alan Hansen. I was buzzing after enjoying Saturday's game so I didn't mind. Steve Nicol couldn't believe it. 'How come you're the lucky one who always gets a rest?' he joked. John Aldridge scored our goal but David Oldfield equalised for Luton. The main concern is over Gary Gillespie and Nigel Spackman. They clashed heads and both needed treatment for cuts. There is obviously some doubt whether they'll be fit for Saturday.

SATURDAY, 14th MAY

Liverpool 0 Wimbledon 1 (FA Cup final at Wembley)

One of the great sporting occasions of the year. I've watched it on television so often but never been to Wembley for a Cup final before today. Walking out of the tunnel onto the Wembley pitch amid the roar of 98,000 fans was every bit as exhilarating as I'd imagined, and there seemed to be Liverpool fans everywhere. We hoped to give them a day to remember but it didn't work out that way and Wimbledon went away with the Cup and the glory.

For a moment I thought I'd scored. As Gary Gillespie took a quick free-kick I made a run and got away from Andy Thorn, the Wimbledon defender. He tried to hold me back but I was past him and clear with only the goalkeeper to beat. I saw Dave Beasant come out and guessed that he'd go down and spread himself to try to smother the shot. Sure enough Dave did as I expected so I chipped the ball over him into the goal and turned to celebrate with my team-mates. Instead I saw the referee had given us a free-kick and was standing in the place where Andy Thorn had tried to pull me back. I hadn't heard the whistle and couldn't believe that the goal was disallowed.

Within minutes Wimbledon were ahead. Dennis Wise took a free-kick on the edge of the area and Lawrie Sanchez glided his header across the goal and in at the far post. It seemed as though there was plenty of time to get back into the game but we never really got going. Wimbledon packed their defence and we weren't able to break them down. Their goalkeeper, Dave Beasant, was having a good game, and when he saved John Aldridge's penalty it started to look as though it wasn't going to be our day.

I felt so sorry for John. He'd scored from every penalty before the Cup final. At penalties the pressure is always on the man taking the kick to score. The keeper isn't expected to save it and becomes a hero if he does! John was substituted immediately after the kick so he didn't even have time to try to make amends.

We didn't play as well as we could. The grass on the Wembley pitch was very long and the ball didn't run as smoothly as we'd have liked but that's hardly an excuse for a team that have won the championship. It was just one of those games, and Wimbledon deserve credit for the way they played.

The idea that they were a bunch of thugs isn't true. They've attracted a bad reputation and people say they kick and intimidate opponents but I don't agree with that. They have never caused me any trouble, and players like Andy Thorn and Eric Young, who were marking me, were both fair. I don't remember getting kicked in any of our three meetings over the season.

The Wimbledon team were shouting things in the tunnel before the game. If it was an attempt to intimidate us then it didn't work. I caught Alan Hansen's eye while this was going on and we both laughed. A few of their players were making comments in midfield but again we're experienced enough to cope with that and laugh it off.

I'm lucky in being able to get over defeat quite quickly. I was bitterly disappointed when we got back in the dressing room. I'd expected Ronnie Moran to have a go at us for not playing but he was brilliant. 'Don't worry lads,' he said. 'There's only nine weeks until we start pre-season training again.'

119

He did well to cheer us up and tried to lift the spirits. 'We've lost a football match not a war. You've had a brilliant season and no-one can take that away from you.'

Afterwards I learned that Sandra had been through a terrible day as well. The coach taking the players' wives to Wembley had arrived late and she'd been caught up in the crush as fans without tickets tried to force their way in.

But although it was a disappointing end to the season at least we've been there. Jan Molby made a magnificent gesture after the game. He was one of our substitutes but gave his medal to Mike Hooper. It was Mike's vital save at Stoke in the third round that kept us in the competition. Jan reckoned that save was as important in helping us get to the final as anything else during our cup run.

And as Ronnie Moran said – there are only nine weeks before pre-season training and we can start all over again.

12
MY TOP TEAM

Each season the Professional Footballers Association asks its members to nominate not only their player of the year but the best 11 to form a hypothetical super-team.

It always causes arguments in the newspapers and lively discussion among players and football fans across the country. I'm lucky enough to have played with, and against, some of the best footballers not only in Britain but across the world. When it comes to choosing my all time favourite team I think that makes the choice even harder rather than easier. There are so many good players around it's almost impossible to narrow them down for the final 11. I've thought long and hard, written down names that have seemed dead certainties and then crossed them out when I've remembered someone else, and agonised over my final choice A manager's job isn't easy, even when you're only picking a hypothetical team, so I hope I don't offend anyone by leaving them out.

If I start from the back, the goalkeeper I admire the most is Peter Shilton. He won his first England cap in 1971. I was only ten years old at the time and he became one of my schoolboy heroes. After training with him and playing with him I think he's probably the best goalkeeper there's ever been.

Everything about him is outstanding. His attitude to the game is an example to everyone. He takes his training seriously and is annoyed if he lets a goal in during a practice match. To most players practice games don't really matter but Peter is so determined to be the best that he never lets up.

Before I joined Liverpool I'd only scored past him once and that was from a penalty when Newcastle played Southampton on the opening day of the 1985–86 season. I sent him the wrong way, which was very pleasing from my point of view. When you're facing a goalkeeper like Peter Shilton it can be rather daunting as you're always aware that you're up against the best. Unless you do everything right there's every chance he'll save it.

It's rare for Peter Shilton to be beaten when a forward is through and it's one against one. Some keepers go down early giving the forward the chance to go round them. Peter always forces the attacker to make the first move and he's quick enough to react to whatever they do.

When Peter releases the ball he makes it easy for the outfield players to receive. He knows exactly when to release the ball early and when to slow the game down after the team has been under pressure. Instead of booting the ball upfield he'll take his time and calm everyone down.

If Peter Shilton is the best, then Bruce Grobbelaar isn't far behind. Bruce pulls off some incredible saves and gets to balls that look to have beaten him. His ability to read situations around the edge of the penalty area is unrivalled. The way Liverpool play, the defence is often square, but they hold a line which gives Bruce the chance to be first to any through ball. He's so quick that it's like having an extra defender. Supporters love Bruce and his dashes out of his area always add to a game's excitement and keep the crowd entertained.

Bruce is never scared to come off his line and he's developed such a good understanding with the Liverpool defence that they know when he's going to come for a ball and they cover the goal behind him. Sometimes we'll have four or five players on the line as Bruce goes out for a cross. Critics say he makes mistakes but they're few and far between. I'd rather have a keeper like Bruce, prepared to come off his line, than one who's static in comparison.

Once again playing in the same team as Bruce has helped me appreciate him even more. And as well as being a great goalkeeper he's also a great entertainer. Wherever I go with Liverpool it seems everybody wants their photograph taken with Bruce – supporters, hotel workers, people at the airport, the lot. He's the kind of character the game needs.

As a forward I know there are some games when you look at the match programme, read through the opposition's line-up and think: 'Oh no, he's not marking me today!'

I know players who think that about the entire Liverpool defence and there are others whose hearts must sink when they see they're up against Terry Butcher. Terry's sheer size is enough to put some forwards off their game. He's six feet four inches tall and weighs more than 14 stone but he's so comfortable on the ball and never seems to be under pressure. He's difficult to beat in the air and hard to get past on the ground – an ideal defender.

After playing with him for England I've seen for myself that he's a good leader and motivator. In the tunnel before a game he terrifies some opponents with his massive presence and loud voice as he psyches himself up.

I prefer to be marked by a big, gangly centre-half, who commits himself to a tackle and gives a little fellow like me the chance to nip past him. Butch is big but he's not gangly, and unlike other defenders of his size it's impossible to make him look clumsy. He waits long enough to force the forward to make the first move and then pounces to take the ball off him.

Paul McGrath is another classy central defender who always makes life difficult for me. He's not only difficult to beat but he uses the ball well and makes the forward work hard to stop him getting into dangerous attacking positions himself. Paul is one of the best for turning defence into attack and can suddenly turn up in his opponents' penalty area and cause all kinds of problems. Once a forward starts worrying about what his marker is up to then it usually takes the edge off his game.

Alan Hansen has been outstanding in the First Division for almost ten years and he's been nominated as one of the best defenders for eight out of nine seasons in the annual PFA awards. When your fellow professionals rate you that highly you must be good. I never understood why Scotland left him out of their World Cup squad in 1986 or why he was never a regular in their team throughout the 1980s.

What's so special about Alan is that he's never under pressure, no matter how tight the situation, and that is worth a lot in international football. When I was with Newcastle I always found Alan difficult to play against. If you're running at him he tries to force you to take him on early, well away from the goal. It's always tempting to try because if you pass him there's only the goalkeeper to beat but, having said that, it's very rare that anyone actually gets past Alan.

I like defenders to be good footballers, able to win the ball cleanly and use it intelligently. I don't have much time for players who give away needless free-kicks, especially around the edge of the penalty area. With some of the free-kick specialists playing today you're always likely to be punished.

I've been lucky in that I've never been marked by out and out thugs. There are a few in the League, more so in the lower divisions. But when I was at Carlisle I always played alongside a big centre-forward. The 'hard man' defender would normally mark him and leave me relatively unscathed.

There are some players who try to intimidate opponents by muttering things like 'I'm going to snap your legs' and similar threats. I have a moan from time to time if I think things are getting out of hand but I'm lucky to have the temperament which means I don't react. I'm not unsettled by tough talk and I think that once your opponent resorts to that then you know you've got him worried.

Viv Anderson gets my vote at right-back. Because he's so tall, a shade over six feet, some people say he's gangly, but I've played with him and against him and it's very rare for a winger to get past him. When Viv is beaten, he recovers well and his legs are so long that he's often able to hook the ball away or win it back with a sliding tackle. He's good coming forward and his height causes problems for the opposition when he pushes up for corners and free-kicks.

Kenny Sansom has been the first choice left-back for England for most of the 1980s. He's a great character and a marvellous footballer. He's rarely beaten when he's defending and he links well with his own attack.

Steve Nicol seems to have played everywhere for Liverpool from right-back to left-wing and he always looks comfortable in any position. In my first season with Liverpool Steve was outstanding. Again he's rarely beaten and looks dangerous when he goes forward.

Everyone at Anfield was sad that Mark Lawrenson's career was prematurely ended by injury. He was only 30 when he retired midway through my first season with the club. He was always hard to play against, and, although I always fancied my chances of taking Mark on and getting past him, he was so quick to recover that I could never get away.

People talk about Franz Beckenbauer as the ideal model for a defender. I played against Franz in America when he was probably past his best and was just passing time. He played sweeper although he rarely came forward and never passed the ball more than ten yards. It was sad that time had caught up with him but in the 1970s he was an outstanding player.

If I had to choose my ideal midfield player I would go for Bryan Robson. He defends well and attacks well and is always capable of scoring. He covers so much ground during a game and is an inspiration to his team-mates.

I'm also a great fan of Paul Gascoigne. I first noticed him when he was about 14 years old and he came along to Newcastle as a schoolboy. We all knew the club thought he was special because they asked Kevin Keegan to work with him in training. He had so much ability, and even at that age he would hold his own in practice matches with the reserves.

When he broke into the first team he was a sensation. His strength is going forward. At Newcastle he would start a move in our half and invariably be in a position to finish it off in the opponents' penalty area. He could see things that no-one else could see, not even people with the best seat in the ground. He's such a positive player that he's always thinking about attack.

Critics say he's too cocky and defensively naive. When I was with him at Newcastle he was willing to argue with anyone. He's so talented that he didn't always respect players who weren't blessed with his ability. Players with experience often know what to do, even if they can't get their feet into action as quickly as someone like Paul. He used to think people were picking on him when they were trying to help.

The defensive side of his game needs to be worked on. Paul was so intent on going forward that he would never see opponents break from midfield. Paul would often be left standing while his opposite number burst unmarked into our penalty area.

But that part of his game will improve with experience and Paul compensates with his strength in attack. I've always been convinced that Paul will be one of the best in the world.

Alongside Bryan Robson and Paul Gascoigne I'd pick Ray

Wilkins. He's the best captain I've ever played for and in my opinion he's the best passer of the ball in the game.

If you stood Ray on the centre-spot and asked him to hit a ball to any part of the pitch, any distance, the pass would be inch perfect. And he can do it with either foot. Even when he's having a poor game, Ray will never hide. He's always looking to receive the ball, never looks under pressure and always helps the players around him and brings them into the game.

Ray's had his share of critics. They say he doesn't tackle and hits too many square passes. That criticism is not only unfair, it ignores the impact he has on his team-mates and the game. At Manchester United I saw at first hand how good a motivator he can be. Admittedly it wasn't for many games, my one first team appearance and a handful of reserve matches when he was coming back from injury, but everything about Ray was class and he inspired team-mates to some great performances.

Ray also scored some marvellous goals. The one that sticks in my mind was in the 1983 FA Cup final against Brighton. He received a pass on the right wing, cut inside his man and measured his chip perfectly to beat the Brighton keeper, Graham Moseley, on the far post.

He's so talented, has such good ideas about the game and is such a good motivator that I'm sure he'll go on to become a successful manager.

Glenn Hoddle is one of the most skilful players I'ver ever seen. His killer pass is from the right wing to the far post where Glenn can pick out his man, even if that man is tightly marked. Glenn will drop the ball over the defender's head and into his team-mate's path. Time and again I've seen defenders who are marking man-to-man stretch in vain to cut out one of Glenn's passes only to see the ball fall perfectly for the player they're marking.

Glenn set up my first goal for England. We were playing Mexico in Los Angeles as part of the warm up to the 1986 World Cup. He chipped a ball onto my chest which fell so sweetly that I didn't need to control it. All I had to do was turn and shoot and I'd scored my first goal in an international.

Critics say Glenn can't tackle but if you've got the ability he's got it more than compensates. And with a ball winner alongside him he can be devastating. Glenn was magnificent in the Mexico World Cup when he moved into the centre of midfield. There was one memorable moment against Paraguay where he went to play a ball with his right foot, fooled the entire Paraguayan defence and then played a perfect pass with the outside of his left foot into Gary Stevens' path. Gary crossed for Gary Lineker to score but it had all been created by that memorable piece of skill from Glenn. It was as though he had both feet in the air at the same time and it's the kind of skill you can't teach.

There's nobody in the game who can bring the ball under control as well as Glenn. You can hit the ball at him at any angle or any height and he'll bring it under control with his first touch. Having such a good first touch gives him that extra time to move into space or lay off a pass. I appreciate players with skill and it's a joy to watch Glenn in action.

I'd love to pack my ideal side with ball-players, the kind of footballer who's going to entertain the crowd. Jinky Jimmy Smith was a great example and my first football hero when I was a young fan at Newcastle United. George Best was another hero. I saw him a few times when Manchester United came to Newcastle, and I remember one match when they beat us 5–1 and he was outstanding.

I was lucky enough to play against George in North America and he still showed flashes of his old skill. He wasn't a big man but nobody seemed to be able to knock him off the ball. Keegan and Dalglish seem to be well built with plenty of muscle but although George looked relatively frail he took a tremendous buffeting and still kept his feet and the ball. He had marvellous balance and was able to ride tackles with ease. And he played the game fairly. Despite all the provocation he received I don't remember him looking for penalties and free-kicks by diving.

John Barnes is blessed with similar skill. He's bigger than George but is still able to glide past the roughest of tackles. He has an even temperament, which is just as well when you receive the treatment John does. And his personality is such that he always works very hard for the team.

Chris Waddle is another player who loves to run at defenders. He's a one-off. I was lucky to play alongside him in Newcastle's promotion season when he was magnificent. Defenders didn't have an answer to him. Chris would step over the ball one way, then the other, and although the ball hadn't moved he would have sent the defender the wrong way every time.

He's always looked as though he's shattered, with drooped shoulders and hands on hips as if he won't last another five minutes. In fact, he's one of the fittest players in the England squad. When we went through some tests for heart-beat, recovery times and general fitness before the Mexico World Cup Chris was easily the fittest.

Like me Chris had a late chance to break into professional football. He was a factory worker before Newcastle discovered him and it makes you wonder how many other talented players are waiting for the right opportunity.

I've never played with a better goalscorer than Gary Lineker. If he gets a chance, no matter how difficult, you can safely bet that nine times out of ten Gary will hit the target. They may not all go in but at least he'll force the goalkeeper to make a save.

Gary's greatest asset is his speed. The biggest worry for any defence is a forward's pace, and Gary is so quick that he gets beyond his markers before they have time to respond.

I work well with Gary because our styles complement each other. He likes to be in and around the penalty area while I prefer to play a bit deeper. I like to knock balls through for players to run on to and Gary likes to chase balls played in like that.

I also rate Clive Allen very highly. He's an excellent goalscorer. People say he doesn't work during a game but defenders can never afford to leave him unmarked. Like Gary Lineker, if there's a chance going begging Clive will be in with a shot. He's been unlucky that the chances haven't fallen for him when he's played for England. His 49 goals for Tottenham in the 1986–87 season is proof enough for me that he's one of the best forwards around.

I also like Mark Hateley because he's good in the air and so difficult to knock off the ball. He's also got one of the hardest shots in the game. I've been in goal a few times when we've been mucking about in training with England, and Mark's shots have been so hard I've never got anywhere near them.

Mark is an ideal target man. Once the ball is knocked up to him he can shield it and hold up play for ages until support arrives. He is so strong that defenders are unable to push him off the ball.

My team would have to include Kenny Dalglish. When I was young he was my biggest hero. I'm not saying that because he became my boss (honestly!), but when I was in my early teens Celtic were my favourite Scottish team and Kenny was their star player at the time. I used to pretend to be him when we played games over the park and I never imagined that he'd eventually be my boss.

He deserves to be included in any list of all time greats. When he joined Liverpool he faced a difficult task in replacing Kevin Keegan. Some said it was impossible and that Keegan was irreplaceable but Kenny proved them wrong and became an even greater hero on Merseyside.

I played against him three or four times and every time he impressed me more. He has the ability to do things that no other player can do. There were times when he seemed to be drifting out of position and out of the game. I remember thinking 'What's he doing there?' then suddenly he would receive the ball and with his first touch he would hit a pass which opened our defence and set free one of his team-mates.

His vision is incredible and he has so many tricks such as back-heels, flicks and so on that his marker is often caught by surprise. There is one goal that sticks in my mind where Kenny created the chance out of nothing for Ian Rush. Liverpool were playing Watford and the ball was played to the by-line. Kenny chased after it followed closely by a Watford defender, but Kenny sold such a good dummy the defender carried on and went off the pitch while Kenny spun inside him and set up a lovely pass for Ian Rush to score. It was such an enjoyable moment and I would love to be able to fool defenders in that way.

Kenny is only slightly bigger than I am but he was able to look after himself when the game became physical. There are times when I wish I was more like that. He did things that no-one expected from a little man and thought nothing of blocking players when they tried to get round him. There are traces of a mean streak in Kenny and there are times when I wish I had a similar streak in my game.

If I was allowed two players from abroad then I'd choose Ruud Gullit and Diego Maradona. As they're two of the most expensive players in the world they're hardly surprise choices.

Gullit is capable of scoring some marvellous goals and pops up all over the pitch helping and encouraging his team-mates. He seems adaptable and would fit in with the free flowing style I'd like my ideal team to adopt.

Maradona would get in nine out of ten teams from any era. He's got so much skill and when he starts to dribble the ball looks as though it's attached to his boot. During the 1986 World Cup he was probably the best individual player, always looking to take on defenders and try the unexpected. But I was disappointed to see him start moaning when the ball didn't come his way. I prefer players to be constructive rather than whinge for 90 minutes. And I was disappointed to see him look for free-kicks. He took some fierce and wild tackles which he rode beautifully but the next moment he'd take a dive, even though the defender had never touched him.

But without those two I would still be able to select an excellent side with players from the British Isles. As manager I would put skill first and go for players that are blessed with exceptional talent but also work hard for their team.

It's impossible to choose 11 when you've got the pick of the best. There are so many good players that I haven't even mentioned who would probably be first choice in other people's teams. But if I was pressed I would select the following 11, picked on individual merit but also with the knowledge that they would form a balanced team: SHILTON, ANDERSON, HANSEN, McGRATH, NICOL, GASCOIGNE, ROBSON, WILKINS, BARNES, LINEKER, and DALGLISH.

13
THE EUROPEAN
CHAMPIONSHIPS

My first season with Liverpool had finished on a disappointing note, losing to Wimbledon in the FA Cup final, but there was plenty of football to look forward to before Sandra and I went off for our summer holidays. The European Championships in West Germany were less than a month away and the England management had arranged a series of warm-up matches for us before setting off for our base near Stuttgart and our challenge for football's most important trophy after the World Cup.

We went into the championships as one of the favourites. Our record was easily the best of the seven nations who'd had to qualify and the experts were tipping ourselves and West Germany as the two teams most likely to win the tournament. Our first round group in Germany included the Republic of Ireland, Holland and the Soviet Union. The teams were to play each other once in a mini-league with the top two sides going through to the semi-finals against the top two teams from the other group which included West Germany, Denmark, Spain and Italy.

The England players were looking forward to the competition, my confidence was high after that incredible season with Liverpool and we felt sure that we would do well. The nucleus of the squad had been together since the Mexico World Cup two years earlier. We felt we'd improved since then and were ready to mount a serious challenge in Germany.

The team had qualified for the finals in style winning five of our six matches. We'd scored 18 goals and conceded only one – the best defensive record in all the qualifying groups. In our final qualifying match we'd won 4–1 away to Yugoslavia in one of our best performances for some time. We seemed set to build on that and go on to greater things.

Unfortunately it all went horribly wrong. We lost all three first round matches and finished bottom of our group. Instead of playing in the final in Munich I ended up watching it on television at home.

Everything had gone so well before the competition. We played a series of friendlies beating Scotland 1–0 at Wembley, drawing 1–1 with Columbia and then winning 1–0 away to Switzerland where once again I'd combined with Gary Lineker for the only goal of the game. I broke free from the half-way line before passing across the edge of the penalty area for Gary to shoot first time past the Swiss keeper. It was a beautifully taken goal.

The manager, Bobby Robson, was disappointed that we hadn't scored more but we were pleased that we were playing well and creating chances even if they weren't all going in.

It had been a similar story against Scotland where I'd scored the only goal. We created a number of openings but on the day the Scottish goalkeeper Jim Leighton was inspired and pulled off some incredible saves.

It was important to get through these games and get used to playing with each other again. In between matches Don Howe took some tough training sessions. It was hard but a lot of the lads had been off for ten or 12 days since the end of the season and didn't mind a good work out – it was only the Liverpool players who'd been in action more recently in the Cup Final.

We played one more friendly before leaving for Germany, a match against the Beazer League champions Aylesbury, which we won comfortably. I enjoyed myself and scored four.

Practise matches like that are often better than training sessions. Players who haven't had a game for a while get a run out and it helps you get used to playing alongside different team-mates.

We had another practise game in Germany against a fourth division side, VFR Hollbrein. It was a lovely, warm afternoon with a sizeable crowd, made up mostly of families, and there wasn't a hint of trouble. The match was played in Guglingen, a small town to the north of Stuttgart. It was a big day for them and a worthwhile exercise for us. We won 4–0, had a good work out and made plenty of friends. We picked up a couple of minor injuries but nobody was complaining as they could happen just as easily in a training session.

We went back to our hotel in Ludwigsburg to prepare for our opening game against the Republic of Ireland the following Sunday. Everything seemed set for a successful championships but it wasn't to be.

The England v Ireland game provided probably the biggest shock of the tournament. Ray Houghton's goal gave the Republic a 1–0 win which left the Irish fans jubilant and English supporters in a state of shock. We'd been expected to win quite easily, even though Ireland had a number of experienced First Division footballers in their team, including Paul McGrath, and my Liverpool team-mates Ray Houghton, Ronnie Whelan and John Aldridge.

We'd gone into the game in good spirits. Everyone was confident and even after we went 1–0 down to Ray Houghton's goal after eight minutes I don't believe any of us thought we would lose. But we couldn't get going in the first half and rarely troubled the Irish defence. It was a different story in the second half and we created enough chances to have won easily. In the end I missed a couple and Pat Bonner, in the Irish goal, made some excellent saves. I doubt if he has ever played better. He blocked everything we threw at him, even stopping one shot with his chin!

Glenn Hoddle came on as substitute and was magnificent. He hit one shot, a volley from the edge of the area followng a corner, which would have been the goal of the tournament had it gone in. Instead it shaved the post.

But despite our pressure we couldn't score. It felt like a repeat of the FA Cup final against Wimbledon just a few weeks earlier. You get the feeling that it's not going to be your day but you have to keep plugging away and hope that your luck will change.

In the last minute Bonner made another point-blank save pushing the ball against the post before it was cleared to safety. It was our last chance to save the match. The luck had been with the Irish but they'd worked hard for their win and Paul McGrath in particular was outstanding.

The lads were obviously disappointed and there were some long faces as we made our way back to the dressing room. The manager was trying to be positive, saying we'd played well and would still qualify if we won our next two games. He pointed out that we'd lost our opening game in the World Cup two years earlier but recovered well enough to win through to the next round.

I had to leave before the post-match inquest. When I got to the dressing room I found that my number had been drawn for the drug test along with Kenny Sansom. It was the last thing I wanted to do. It had been so hot that afternoon and I'd lost so much fluid it took me four hours to deliver my sample. Tony Galvin and Chris Hughton were there from the Irish team and were obviously delighted to have won although they admitted they were surprised at the result.

That four-hour wait gave me plenty of time to reflect on the match and the consequences of the result. We'd made life difficult coming away without a point but I still felt confident that we would get the right results from our next two matches and go through to the semi-finals.

Our next opponents were Holland. They'd been tipped as a good outside bet to win the championships and had some world class players including Ruud Gullit. But, like us, they'd lost their opening match, going down 1–0 to the Soviet Union. That combination of results meant whoever lost in Dusseldorf would be out of the competition.

The match took on the feel of a proper cup tie. The atmosphere inside the Rhine Stadium in Dusseldorf was electric. Thousands of Dutch fans had made their way across the border into Germany for the game and vast sections of the stadium were a mass of orange. It's unfortunate that the hooligans grabbed the headlines in the newspapers as thousands of genuine England fans were also in the stadium and sang their hearts out for us.

The night before the match there had been trouble in the town with German and English youths clashing near the station. The players didn't hear about it until much later. We were staying outside Dusseldorf and were quite cut off. I heard later that gangs of Germans had started the fighting but once again England fans had been involved. The authorities had feared trouble on the day of the game, and there were armed guards on the England team coach on the way to the stadium, but the match passed without incident off the pitch.

On it, we could have been 2–0 up as first Gary Lineker and then Glenn Hoddle, with a magnificent shot from a free-kick, hit the post. But at half-time we found ourselves a goal down. In the 43rd minute Gullit broke on the left wing and played the ball in to Marco Van Basten on the near post. Van Basten was tightly marked by Tony Adams who seemed to have covered any danger. But Van Basten controlled the ball, twisted and swayed to create a space, then span round to shoot into the far corner. It was a beautifully taken goal.

The relief throughout the Dutch side was apparent to us all. Normally it's only the forwards and a few midfield players who join in the celebrations but the entire team was mobbing Van Basten.

Eight minutes into the second half we were level. I knocked a pass into Bryan Robson who played one–two with Gary Lineker, his determination taking him through the heart of the Dutch defence before prodding the ball past Van Breukelen, their goal-keeper. It was one of the best goals of the tournament.

We could see from the looks on their faces that the Dutch players were worried. We were back in the game and had them rattled as we enjoyed our best period of the match. Both sides needed to win but we couldn't push home our advantage.

Then, with 20 minutes to go we found ourselves behind once more as the Dutch again made the most of a lucky break. I headed a ball away from a free-kick but it fell to Jan Wouters on the edge of our area. Wouters mishit his shot but the ball fell nicely for Gullit. Somehow he readjusted his feet so quickly that with one swift shuffle he created the space and angle for a ball to Van Basten – his shot flashing past Shilton.

The third Dutch goal came from a corner, Van Basten complet-ing his hat-trick after Kieft flicked the ball back from the near post. It finished 3–1 to Holland but I thought the scoreline flattered the Dutch. We'd matched them for much of the game and outplayed them in periods but once again we hadn't had the breaks. That's not to take anything away from Van Basten's finishing, which was of the highest class, but for the second game in a row the run of the ball had been against us.

Again the authorities feared trouble after the game so we were smuggled out of the stadium through a back entrance to avoid the fans. Instead of leaving in our normal England team bus, we went back to our hotel in an unmarked coach.

Two defeats in two games meant we were out of the competition. So much had been expected but things hadn't gone our way. The manager did his best to lift our spirits. He said we'd played well, that our attitude had been good and that we hadn't had the breaks. And he said we still had a chance to restore our pride by beating the Soviet Union in our final game.

None of us wanted to go out losing three games in a row and there was the added incentive that a victory over the USSR might help the Irish to qualify for the semi-finals.

In the event the boss left me out of the side for the final game. He'd taken me off in the matches against Ireland and Holland, pushing Mark Hateley on in my place. I was disappointed but appreciated that Mark would give the team a different option. He's strong in the air and causes problems for defenders and if Mark had scored no-one would have been happier than me.

On the day before the USSR match, the manager called me to one side after training. He asked how I was feeling and said he thought I looked tired. I guessed he was thinking about leaving me out. I wanted to play but on the morning of the match he called me over for another chat. 'I'm sorry but I'm leaving you out today,' he said. 'You've had such a hard season with Liverpool where everybody wants to beat you and you're under such pressure all the time, that I'm going to give you a rest.'

He said Glenn Hoddle would take my place with the freedom to float around. I was disappointed of course. Like the other lads I wanted another chance to go some way towards putting things right, salvage some pride and show that we could play. But I respected his reasons and the fact that he took time to explain things to me.

I was one of the substitutes for the USSR game and although they dominated the first 15 minutes or so we came back into the game and could have been 2–1 up. Tony Adams put us level with a header from a Glenn Hoddle free-kick and then John Barnes whipped in a great cross to the far post. Trevor Steven got up to meet it, his downward header beating Daseyev but bouncing up and off the bar.

Instead the Soviet Union went 2–1 up through Mikhailichenko and added a third in the second half, a cross from the left wing going in off Tony Adams and the substitute Pasulko.

Three defeats in three games sounds as if we were comprehensively beaten. But I honestly believe we played well enough in our first two games to qualify for the semi-finals. I know we could have played better and should have taken some of the chances we created in those first two matches. But both games were entertaining and we put together some fine moves.

People have said that I looked tired in those matches but I felt fine. I'd had a tough season but that's not an excuse and the adrenalin of being involved in such an important tournament keeps you going. I felt I was always involved in the game, either making runs to look for the ball, runs to take defenders away and create space for a team-mate or runs to get back and cover an opponent. Teams and players go through periods where they don't get the run of the ball and unfortunately that happened to us at the wrong time.

John Barnes came in for criticism but the opposition know what a good player he is and had two men on him in each game. Against Holland, Van Aerle never left his side with Vanenburg dropping back to cover at the first hint of danger. The way the Dutch play, with so many players filling in so many different positions, meant they always had cover when they defended. A lot of continental teams play a sweeper which allows other defenders to push forward and mark man-to-man. Both Gary Lineker and I had markers with us for most of the tournament with the full-backs pushing up to mark our wingers. Gary's pace took him clear when balls were played into space, but John Barnes and I received the ball to feet, with a marker on our back immediately.

You don't get that in the First Division. With no sweepers, teams can't afford to push defenders forward to mark opponents lying deep as there's no-one to cover behind them.

Despite the close marking John still caused problems for defenders. He didn't get in as many crosses as he would have liked but he never gave up. I shared a room with him throughout the tournament and I know he was disappointed we didn't do better. John suffers terribly from hay-fever and was up all night, sneezing and wheezing, coughing and spluttering. Because of the strict controls on drugs he wasn't able to take any medication. He never complained but it was obvious to me that he was shattered.

It was obvious too that Gary Lineker was off colour. His wife, Michelle, had come out to Germany to watch the tournament and was travelling from match to match with Sandra. The boss let us go off to see them both for an hour the day after the Holland match. I could tell that Gary was feeling below par although none of us

137

realised that his illness was so serious until I heard later that he'd gone for tests for hepatitis after the tournament. It says a lot for Gary that he did so well and got into so many good positions even though he wasn't feeling his best.

Inevitably there are lessons to be learned from our defeats but the hysterical outcry from some sections of the press was way over the top and the attacks on the manager unfair and at times outrageous. A few months earlier the papers had been raving over our win in Yugoslavia, now the same people were saying the same players couldn't play.

The lads were disgusted at the hammering the boss took. If anything it united the team even more behind the manager. The level of criticism was way out of proportion to what happened. To read some of the stories you would think we had commited a terrible crime rather than lose three football matches. No-one was more disappointed than the players but it's not the end of the world.

And we weren't that far away from winning. If we'd taken our chances against Ireland we could have settled for a draw against Holland rather than push forward for the win and leave ourselves open at the back. And if the luck had been with us against Holland we might well have won that match as well.

I think maybe we were too worried about what the critics were saying. In Mexico I was there for the ride and determined to enjoy every minute but in Germany there was more pressure on us because we were one of the favourites.

My biggest disappointment was for the fans. The press concentrated on those who caused trouble but that doesn't mean that all fans are yobs and thugs. There were thousands of genuine well behaved footbal supporters who scimped and saved and paid a lot of money to come and see us. We were sorry we let them down.

It's unfortunate that the behaviour of the hooligans gives all supporters a bad name as I'm sure the vast majority just want to have a good time. After the game against Ireland, Kenny Sansom and I didn't get away from the stadium until late becuse we were called in for the drug test. The rest of the lads had gone on to Dusseldorf and we had to follow with the team doctor by minibus. I was so hungry that we stopped for a hamburger in McDonalds where we met an Irish fan wearing a green shirt with 1–0 painted

on his forehead. He'd obviously been celebrating and was astonished to see two England players walk in. Once he'd recovered he
was incredibly friendly. He said he was having a marvellous trip
and was in a bar down the road with Irish and English fans having
a good time together, just the way it should be.

I'm sure there were similar stories all over Germany, it's just
unfortunate that a few hooligans can spoil it for the well behaved
fans.

I watched the rest of the tournament on television at home. As
far as I'm concerned Italy was the best team. They were magnificent until the semi-final when they lost to the Soviet Union.
Vialli and Mancini looked a dangerous partnership up front, their
midfield interchanged well, the left-back Maldini was one of the
players of the tournament and the sweeper Franco Baresi was
magnificent.

Their form in the early games had suggested they could go on to
win the competition but they slipped up against the Soviet side
where their flair and imagination deserted them. The USSR
deserved to win on the night. They took the game to the Italians,
had the best of the first half and scored twice in the second half for
a 2–0 win.

It was a strange tournament with results often going against
form. The USSR struggled against Ireland and escaped with a
fortunate draw and they should have lost to Holland in their
opening game but won. Teams were playing badly and getting
through, then playing well and losing.

I'm pleased that Holland went on to win the tournament. Van
Basten was again instrumental in both their semi-final win against
West Germany and in the final against the USSR. His winner
against Germany was superbly taken, chasing a ball played into
the inside right channel and then sliding it past the keeper at the
far post.

Holland had been behind in that game and drew level after a
controversial penalty. The referee ruled that Kohler had brought
down Van Basten. It looked a harsh decision to me and to be fair to
Van Basten he tried to get up and continue playing – other players
might have been tempted to play for the penalty but I was
impressed by his honesty.

In the end Holland and the USSR, who'd both beaten England,
met in the final in Munich. Fittingly it was Gullit and Van Basten

who scored the goals that gave Holland a 2–0 win. Van Basten's shot will be remembered for a long time to come – a right-foot volley from the edge of the penalty area which flashed past Dasayev, the Soviet keeper, into the far corner of the net. It had the mark of a world class player and showed how confident he must have felt to even try such a shot.

But the tournament will also be remembered for the Irish. They came within nine minutes of reaching the semi-finals, going out to a fluke goal by the Dutch substitute Kieft, his header from a mishit shot from Koeman spinning past Bonner into the goal. There was even a question that one of the Dutch players was off-side but the goal stood to see the Dutch through and mark the end of the Irish challenge.

I was pleased they did so well. I'd had my differences with the Irish manager Jack Charlton when we were at Newcastle, but he did a superb job in Germany. And I was delighted for my Liverpool team-mates John Aldridge, Ray Houghton and Ronnie Whelan. They all proved they were quality international players and Ronnie's goal against the USSR was one of the best of the season.

We didn't get a chance to chat during the tournament, only having time for a quick hello and good luck in the tunnel before the England v Ireland game. But afterwards they were full of praise for Jack Charlton. He was so relaxed about everything that they were able to enjoy every moment of the tournament.

Ray Houghton had a superb championship. In many ways the Irish system wasn't suited to him. They played plenty of long balls up to their forwards, by-passing the midfield, but Ray still managed to dictate the play and was outstanding in every match.

Other players who caught my eye included Flemming Povlsen, the Danish forward, who looks to have a bright future and Miguel Soler, the Spanish defender, who came on as substitute for Camacho against Denmark and played in their 1–0 defeat against Italy. He looked good going forward and seemed to be a fine defender.

Lothat Matthus, the West German captain, was strong and hard in midfield but few players could match Bryan Robson's performance. He was outstanding in all three England games and deserved better reward than to be on the losing side so early.

From England's point of view it was a disappointing tournament but I don't believe that our game is as bad as some critics would have us believe. I think we missed Terry Butcher more than we feared. That's not taking anything away from the players at the back, but Terry is so experienced and organises the defence so well that he makes sure everything is covered. He plays the ball out of defence well and rarely wastes a pass, knocking long and accurate balls up for the midfield and forwards. His absence was more costly than I'd imagined it would be.

It's hard to explain why things went so wrong. Perhaps the build up had gone too well and we became complacent. If you're going to have problems it's better to have them before a major tournament and get them out of the way. Italy, for example, lost at home to Wales a few weeks before they went to Germany and then went on to play some great football. Unfortunately every England game is under such scrutiny that there's never a moment when the team can afford to slip up. If an experiment fails the critics are quick to jump in and say that we're not up to it.

But one thing was certain. The England players who flew home early from Germany were more determined than ever to prove their critics wrong. Bobby Robson had steered us through qualifying rounds for the World Cup in 1986 and the 1988 European Championships. We knew we should have done better once we reached those finals and there was a new determination to put things right for the next World Cup in Italy in 1990.

14
HILLSBOROUGH

I'll never forget the 15th April 1989. Nor will anyone else connected with Liverpool Football Club. What should have been a day of footballing celebration ended in tragedy with 95 people being crushed to death at the FA Cup semi-final between Liverpool and Nottingham Forest at Hillsborough.

The full horror of that day will probably never go away for some people. No inquiries will ever bring back those who died but for football's sake I hope that lessons were learned and every effort made to ensure that such a disaster will never happen again.

For many of the Liverpool players that day changed the way they think. It put life into perspective and made us value those things that are really important. The disappointment of the European Championships was no longer a disaster for English football as far as I was concerned – not when the reality of disaster had happened before my very eyes.

Hillsborough dominated the season. It made everyone in the game sit up and think about the way we treat the fans. And it proved to me that the people of Liverpool are unique, as they rallied round each other with support, comfort and warmth.

The season had been going so well for Liverpool. It had started with a sensation – the return of Ian Rush for £2.8 million after just a year with the Italian club Juventus. None of the players had an inkling that he was coming back. It came as a huge surprise.

As the start of the season approached there had been talk of us signing another defender. The grapevine was buzzing with the name Gary Pallister, then with Middlesbrough. On the Thursday before the FA Charity Shield match Kenny Dalglish slipped away from training a few minutes early. One of the lads saw him get into his car wearing a suit – which was most unusual and indicated that either he was going to a board meeting or about to sign someone.

I thought nothing more about it and went home as usual and had a sleep in the afternoon. When I woke up there was one dream that was fresh in my mind. I told Sandra that I'd dreamed we'd signed Ian Rush. We both laughed about it but then I remembered one of the fans outside Anfield that day asking if it was true that Ian was coming back to play for Liverpool. The idea seemed far fetched, but the dream had been so vivid. So, to put my mind at rest, I turned on the TV and checked the teletext. And there, large as life was the main sport story: RUSH REJOINS LIVERPOOL.

I was shocked. The players hadn't suspected and I was amazed that Ian had decided to come back to Liverpool so quickly. His arrival would strengthen our squad and the lads were delighted to have him back. Only John Barnes, Ray Houghton and myself had never played with him before, but the others knew what he could do. We'd done so well without him the previous year, the feeling was that with Ian back there was nothing to stop us winning the lot.

Ironically, we made a poor start to the season. And just when we should have been finding our form we hit a terrible run. We lost at home to Newcastle and away to Luton and Nottingham Forest. We were also held to a goalless draw at Anfield by Coventry and suffered the taunts of their fans as they revelled in our poor performance chanting 'You're not the champions anymore.' We'd lost three out of four games in October, slipped to sixth in the League and were losing touch with the surprise leaders, Norwich and Millwall.

Our poor form coincided with a run of injuries to key players. John Barnes missed five games with a hamstring injury, Gary Gillespie hurt his knee ligaments and Bruce Grobbelaar, Alan Hansen and Steve McMahon also missed lengthy spells. By the end of October we'd been unable to field the same team in consecutive games.

Other clubs, expecting the highest standards at all times, may have panicked. Not Liverpool. There was so much experience at the club that the management never lost confidence in our ability. They believed that if we did the correct things it would all come right in the end. They knew that once our game started to come together and we started to play to our potential we would pick up the points. Even at our lowest point they believed we would be challenging for the major honours at the end of the season.

In a sense we were paying for being successful. Teams came to Anfield and were happy to sit back and defend, hoping to steal a goal on a breakaway. They didn't feel able to compete in an open match, and if they held on for a draw they would be delighted. Millwall were a good example. On their visit they scored an early goal to go ahead, and instead of trying to build on that, they pulled men back behind the ball, happy to let us do the work while they absorbed the pressure. Steve Nicol did score to make it 1–1 but it was harder and harder to find the space to play the kind of football we liked to play.

Our season didn't really turn round until after Christmas. By then we were out of the Littlewoods Cup, having lost 4–1 at West Ham. That was an extraordinary result. They were struggling near the foot of the First Division while we'd just knocked out Arsenal, the holders, after two replays. Having done the hard work it was frustrating to go out the way we did, but it was one of those nights. From 2–0 down we pulled a goal back and were looking the better side, but then Steve Staunton tried to steer a cross back to our keeper, Mike Hooper, and succeeded only in steering it into his own goal. Then Tony Gale bent in a free-kick to make it 4–1 and one of the cup upsets of the season was complete.

Changes to the way we played meant it was taking me time to settle into my new role for the season. Kenny Dalglish had the luxury of choosing between Ian Rush, John Aldridge and myself to play up front. For a while he played all three of us, with me dropping deeper into more of a midfield role. I was happy to be in the team but was finding it hard to adjust.

It was often said that Ian Rush and John Aldridge were too similar. They both had dark moustaches and scored a lot of goals but they were distinct players despite looking alike. Ian Rush astonished me with his incredible pace. I'd never seen anyone as quick over the first two or three yards. He scored a goal at Derby, where I pulled a ball back from the by-line and he appeared from nowhere to nip in between a Derby defender and Peter Shilton, the Derby goalkeeper. It looked like a simple tap in, but he'd created the chance from nothing with that incredible burst of pace.

144

John Aldridge wasn't as fast but he had a marvellous eye for goal. His game was concentrated in the opposition penalty area. Ian Rush would contribute to the build-up in different parts of the pitch, but John Aldridge knew he was at his most dangerous hanging around the goal area and he had a knack of getting into positions in anticipation of the half-chance.

Ian Rush took a while to get back to his best. He'd been ill during the summer and that had sapped a lot of his strength. And early on, he wasn't getting the breaks. He was often in the right position but goalkeepers were stopping his shots with their legs and other efforts were hitting the crossbar or rebounding off the post. His run of bad luck and near misses was typical of our early form.

But our season probably turned on New Year's Day when we lost to Manchester United. A 3–1 defeat may sound an unlikely springboard for success but we felt we were the better team and hadn't deserved to lose. We took the lead through John Barnes, but then relaxed, allowing United to get back in the game, which they did almost immediately, with Brian McClair scoring their equaliser. That goal gave them the ideal boost and they went on to add two more. But up until that first goal they hadn't troubled us. A moment's lapse had let them back in the game and proved costly.

Games like that can often decide championships. United should have built on that success and put together a good run to be challenging for the First Division title. But they didn't and went on to lose to teams they should have beaten. Liverpool learned their lesson and, boosted by our display that day if not the result, we started an unbeaten run that lasted until the very end of the season.

Our League form in January may not have been spectacular but it laid the foundations for our challenge for the title. We were still a long way adrift of the leaders but in March we started a run of nine League wins on the trot. One of the best performances was away at Middlesbrough, where we won 4–0.

Our display that day came as a surprise. Most of the Liverpool team had been away during the week playing for their countries. John Barnes and I had been to Albania with England for a World Cup qualifying match, and those trips tended to take a lot out of us. But on this occasion there were no ill-effects. On the contrary, the break seemed to have revitalised all of us and we played some of the best football of the season. I scored the opening goal in one of the most satisfying games I've ever played in.

To make it even more enjoyable we got back to the changing rooms to hear that Arsenal, the current League leaders, had lost 3–1 at home to Nottingham Forest. It was the perfect combination of results. We were still 13 points behind Arsenal, but felt confident we could pull it back.

We followed the win at Middlesbrough with a 5–0 victory over Luton in mid-week. John Aldridge hit a hat-trick that night, and as a team we'd scored nine goals in two games. We were finding our form at the right time, and consolidating our position by picking up maximum points each game. With three points for a win, we were racing up the League.

We were also going well in the FA Cup and once again there was the prospect of the League and Cup double. The Cup run had started away to Carlisle, the club that gave me my start as a footballer. I'd watched the draw for the third round on Match of the Day, the evening before we played Everton in a League match. Carlisle had won at Scarborough in the second round, with the match being settled by an own goal. I couldn't imagine a better draw for us. I had so many happy memories of the club, I'd met Sandra there, and her family still lived in the town.

The Carlisle fans gave me a great reception. I hadn't been sure what to expect. Players often go back to their former clubs and are greeted with jeers or chants of rejection from the people who used to support them, but the Carlisle supports had always been special. It was a good day, we won 3–0, but Carlisle were far from disgraced. At the time they were struggling near the bottom of the Fourth Division. This was their big day, they had a large crowd – around 18,000 – and made a lot of money, taking around £75,000 in gate receipts, a club record. I was delighted to see them finish the season with a good run to lift themselves to a comfortable mid-table position.

In the fourth round we were drawn away to Millwall and to my surprise I found myself left out of the team. The manager took Ray Houghton and myself into his room on the morning of the match and explained that he was sacrificing us for the sake of the team.

'We've got a hard job on,' he said, 'but I think this is the best way to approach it.'

Both Ray and myself were bitterly disappointed but there was no argument once the boss had made up his mind. And, as it turned out, it was a master stroke from the manager. He'd picked a team to combat Millwall's game which was based on pumping high balls towards the opposing goal. Alex Watson came in at the back and played as though he'd been in the team all his life. His strength is in the air, and Millwall played to it. Alex won everything that day and second half goals from Aldridge and Rush saw us through.

It made me realise quite how astute Kenny Dalglish could be. He showed that he knew the game inside out and revealed his ability to read other managers' minds better than they can read them themselves. There had been occasions during the season when we'd looked uncomfortable against tall forwards and he sensed that Millwall would try to expose that weakness. By plugging that gap he left Millwall devoid of ideas. They didn't know how to handle us.

I was delighted to see us win, but the trouble with such an effective performance was that I couldn't get back in the team and was substitute again the following week at Newcastle. In the ups and downs of a footballer's life, being out of the Liverpool team meant I also lost my place in the England side. Bobby Robson explained that he couldn't really pick me if I wasn't playing for my club.

But I wasn't as unfortunate as David Burrows, the young left back we'd signed from West Brom. He'd established his place in the Liverpool first team and was doing so well that he was picked for the England Under-21 team to play in Albania. Unlike the full England side, the Under-21s didn't take their own chef. David got food poisoning, missed the next few weeks and lost his place for the rest of the season to Steve Staunton.

No footballer likes being left out of his team. I get as frustrated as anyone but fortunes change swiftly in football and within weeks I was back in from the cold and playing better than I had all season. Wins over Hull and Brentford took us to the semi-finals of the FA Cup and our League form continued to improve with wins away at Norwich and at home to Sheffield Wednesday.

By now we were really flying. I scored twice in the 5-1 win over Wednesday, played on the morning of Grand National day. Morning kick-offs are never popular with the players. The normal match day routine is thrown completely, and instead of a lie-in, players are up at 7.30 am for breakfast to give themselves time to get to the ground. Earlier in the season we'd played Manchester United in a morning game and never really got going. Against Wednesday, though, it was a different story and in the afternoon my day was complete as we went to Aintree for the big race, and I backed the first two winners on the card.

The season was coming nicely to the boil. In midweek we played Millwall again, and again Kenny Dalglish out-thought them. Millwall had expected us to play with the same formation we'd used in the Cup and they altered their formation to cope with that. But Kenny Dalglish is too shrewd and instead we reverted to our normal style, outplayed them and won 2–1 to improve our chances in the League even further.

Once again we were the centre of attention. BBC Television sent a camera crew to our hotel to interview the players about the FA Cup semi-final against Nottingham Forest the following Saturday. Our season was peaking at the right time. The fans, who'd been patient throughout our patchy early season form, were fully behind us. More than 42,000 had turned out for a midweek game against Derby. We felt confident of our chances in the League, and victory over Forest would take us to Wembley and once again give us the chance for the double.

Our minds were concentrated on football and the excitement that the end of the season should have had in store. None of us were prepared for the horror of what was to happen at Hillsborough.

Liverpool were used to big matches and the build-up to the Forest game fell into the usual routine. We went away to an hotel near Sheffield, had a walk down to the paper shop to buy a copy of SHOOT on the afternoon before the match, and on the day of the game woke up to glorious sunshine. Many of us went for another peaceful walk, had a meal and then set off to arrive at the ground about an hour and a half before the kick-off.

There was a big crowd building up, as you would imagine with 53,000 expected at Hillsborough. The supporters seemed in good spirits as they cheered our coach on the way to the ground and at that time there was no hint of any problem.

About four minutes into the game we won a corner. Ray Houghton knocked it short to me around the edge of the Forest penalty area and I hit a volley which crashed against the bar. It was the first time I'd realised that something was wrong. As the ball hit the bar I span round in disappointment and saw a disturbance among the Liverpool supporters behind our goal. It wasn't clear what was happening, but it was quite obvious that something was wrong as people were climbing up the fences and spilling onto the pitch.

None of the players realised how serious it was at that time and as the game continued Forest swept into attack. It was then that I noticed a policeman rushing onto the pitch and heading for the referee. He obviously wanted the game stopped, and the ref tapped our captain, Ronnie Whelan, on the backside and told him to get his team off the pitch.

By now the scene was one of confusion. Police and fans were running onto the pitch and the players didn't know what was going on. To begin with some of the lads thought it was a pitch invasion and it was a while before the full picture emerged. We ran down to the changing rooms but if we'd known then what was happening the players would have stayed to offer their help.

Instead we sat in the dressing room with our boots on, wondering what was going on. The referee put his head round the door and said he hoped to start the game again within 15 minutes. But time passed and nothing happened.

An official called in and asked for Kenny Dalglish to go with him and the Forest manager, Brian Clough to try to calm the crowd. We could hear plenty of shouting, and outside, through the dressing room wall, we could hear ambulance sirens. We began to realise that something terrible had happened but the full horror was only slowly unfolding.

A few fans had found their way into the corridor outside the changing rooms and we could hear the terror in their voices as they kept shouting: 'There's twenty dead!' Another voice said: 'No, there's forty people been killed.'

We were still sitting in our kit, in the dressing room, aware that something awful had happened, but unable to help. At half past four a policeman came in and explained that some people had been killed. He told us about the crush at the Leppings Lane End and told us we should get changed. The game was off.

My first thought was for Sandra and I hurriedly showered and rushed to the players' lounge where I was relieved to see she was safe. The room was hushed, with people gathered around the television. As I arrived BBC1's Grandstand programme switched live to Hillsborough and I heard the reporter explain what had happened.

Many people were dead, and the toll was rising all the time, with hundreds more injured. The full horror started to sink in. The players were numb, yet, because we were watching it on television, it was difficult to realise that we were part of the tragedy.

The journey home that evening was long and silent. I couldn't help thinking how lucky it was that my shot had hit the bar. If it had gone in, the number of casualties could have been even greater, with fans swamping forward as they do when a goal is scored, possibly crushing even more people.

The entire country was touched by the tragedy. By the Sunday morning the death toll had risen again – in the end 95 people were to lose their lives – and the enormity of the disaster became clear.

The players went to a special church service that afternoon and the following morning we visited some of the injured in hospital in Sheffield. Many were in a bad way and some were in coma. One man stood out in my mind. He'd been to the game with his son. His son had died and he'd been crushed. But he hugged both John Barnes and myself and said: 'Go on, win that cup for my son,' and then he started to cry.

The people of Liverpool were incredible. They pulled together from all sides of the city, offering comfort to those who'd suffered. Everyone connected with Liverpool Football Club did what they could. Families were invited in to meet the players and we tried as best we could to help and offer support. I knew from losing my mum a short time before how painful the death of a loved one could be.

Players went to funerals, not out of duty, but because they wanted to show their respect for those who died. Kevin McDonald and I went to the funeral of a 27-year-old fan, who'd left a 25-year-old widow. It was very distressing but the family appreciated our gesture. Kevin and I both wore black suits and black ties, yet all the other mourners had red ties, Liverpool scarves, or other souvenirs from the club. It was as if they were celebrating his love of football.

It made many of us think again about the relationship between the club and the supporters. Kenny Dalglish spoke for many of the players when he said he hadn't realised how important Liverpool Football Club was to the people of the city until the Hillsborough disaster.

Wreathes came into the club from across the country and across the world. More than a million people made a pilgrimage to Anfield and within days the pitch was covered with flowers. It was a moving sight and a week after the disaster there was a memorial service which united Merseyside. Scarves were linked from Goodison Park to Anfield and I was given the honour of tying one of the last scarves at 3.06 pm, exactly a week to the minute after the disaster.

None of the players could contemplate football in the days immediately after the tragedy and the club suspended all our fixtures. There was talk of abandoning the season and initially we all wanted to withdraw from the FA Cup, but as time passed more and more of the victims' relatives were telling us to carry on. That's what their loved ones died for, they said, go and win the Cup for them.

So ten days after the disaster we held a players meeting and voted unanimously to play on. I wanted the Cup to be kept in Merseyside as a memorial to those who'd died. I knew how much death can cost emotionally and financially and perhaps if the Cup had been the centre of a museum the proceeds could have gone to a fund for the long-term support of those who'd suffered.

The city of Liverpool had acted with dignity throughout. I had an early chance to get back to normal, scoring twice in England's 5–0 win against Albania. It had been the right moment for me to start playing again. Other players needed more time and it was fitting that Liverpool's first league game after Hillsborough should be against Everton at Goodison. The 0–0 draw probably cost us the championship, but football was the winner that day, with players and supporters making it a memorable occasion.

The Football League insisted that we finish our fixtures by May 26th which meant we had to squeeze in five League matches, an FA Cup semi-final and a possible final into three weeks.

It was a tall order, especially for a team still traumatised from the events at Hillsborough. Although we'd voted to play on, some, like John Aldridge, said they'd lost all appetite for the game. For others, getting back into the old routine helped them recover from their personal distress.

Forest never really had a chance when we played the semi-final again, this time at Old Trafford. John Aldridge scored twice in a 3–1 victory. It set up a Merseyside final against Everton, which would have made the perfect climax to the season. But the FA refused to put back the date and we had to cram in six more matches in 16 days as we picked up our chase for the double.

Wins against Forest, Wimbledon and QPR kept us on course for the League and before we knew it the FA Cup final was upon us. Because of what had happened at Hillsborough it seemed as if the entire country wanted us to win. Everton were in an awkward position and came into the match very much in our shadow. If they won everyone would feel sorry for us, if they lost everyone would be delighted for us, and nobody would feel sorry for them.

The game was marvellous. John Aldridge put us ahead after four minutes, but Everton refused to give up. A minute from the end, their substitute Stuart McCall, pounced on a loose ball to fire home their equaliser and force the game into extra-time.

So often a goal late in the game gives a team the lift they need. They forget that they're tired and play with renewed vigour. But if you concede a goal after being ahead for much of the game it can be a terrible blow, and fatigue comes to the fore. We could see that Everton had found a second wind but fortunes were to swing even more wildly over the next half-hour.

Extra-time belonged to Ian Rush. He'd come on as substitute for John Aldridge and put us ahead with a moment of brilliance, turning his marker as he controlled a pass from Steve Nicol and shooting with his customary precision.

Seven minutes later McCall again put Everton level, controlling a clearance and volleying past Bruce Grobbelaar. Once again the initiative had swung Everton's way but it was to last just a matter of minutes. John Barnes broke clear down the wing, clipped over a cross and Ian Rush nipped in between two Everton defenders to put us ahead once again.

Everton had done so well to pull back twice, but this time we held on, and could have increased our lead before the final whistle but for some marvellous saves from Neville Southall. It had been a thrilling final, and a fitting tribute to those who'd died.

The only disappointment was a pitch invasion by sections of the crowd after the match which prevented us from going on a lap of honour. Until then it had been a great family occasion. Unfortunately a few fools and others who were over-excited took advantage of the decision to strip away the perimeter fences. The invasion by a few ruined the pleasure for the majority. Both teams were set to go on the lap of honour together, Everton players and Liverpool players arm in arm, in a show of Merseyside unity. Instead the officials told us to get back to the dressing rooms and we left the pitch in dribs and drabs. After a marvellous 120 minutes of football it was a terrible anti-climax.

In the changing rooms, the Cup-winning celebrations were under way. The scenes were a total contrast to those after our defeat against Wimbledon 12 months earlier, and the lads were planning their evening's entertainment. My celebrations were rather different. Much as I wanted to go out with the boys I'd arranged a lift home to Southport immediately after the game so I could get back to be with Sandra who was expecting our first child at any time. She was too far down the pregnancy road to make it to Wembley – she'd wanted to come but the doctors said the excitement wouldn't be good for her, and the way the match turned out they were probably right.

I spent the next four hours travelling up the M1 and M6 with Tony Milligan, a policeman who works at Anfield but had always been a bit of an Everton fan. We were working on converting him, and he was slowly becoming a red.

The journey up the motorway was something I'll never forget. We passed an endless stream of Liverpool fans who seemed surprised to see me in the passenger seat of a Peugeot 205. Many of them were beckoning for me to show them my medal. I felt like a member of the Royal Family – for almost four hours I seemed to be holding my medal up to the window to show our fans. Even the Everton supporters joined in the banter and after the disappointment of the pitch invasion, this was like my own lap of honour. And thanks to Tony I was home in time to watch the game again on Match of the Day that evening and relive every kick.

It must be one of the most satisfying moments of a footballer's life to wake up the morning after winning the FA Cup. In nine years as a professional I'd never been on a cup-winning side. For me the FA Cup has always been the most glamorous of our domestic competitions. It's known across the world and I'd dreamed about winning it since I was a small boy. Liverpool's priority each year is the League, because whoever wins that proves they're the best team over the season, but for pure excitement and romance I'd rather win the FA Cup.

There was little time to reflect on our glory though, as we still faced two more League games in the coming week. I was disappointed to be named as substitute for the match against West Ham on the Tuesday night. But the boss said that as I'd played the full 120 minutes on Saturday he wanted to start with John Aldridge and Ian Rush. They'd both played around 60 minutes each so were likely to be fresher.

The lads played well, and I knew then that I would be a doubtful starter for the final game against Arsenal. I had got on as substitute though, and helped us increase a 2–1 lead to 5–1 by the final whistle. I'd had a hand in three goals and hoped that would be enough to earn me a place, but as training progressed I could tell that the boss wanted to start with Ian and John, which meant I would be substitute.

Never can the final match of the season have been so dramatic. The title would be settled at Anfield that night in the game between the only two teams who could win it. A draw would be enough for us and we could even afford to lose by a single goal and still win the League on goal difference. Arsenal needed to beat us by two clear goals to be champions. They had led the League since Christmas but missed their chance to make sure of the title by losing at home to Derby and then drawing with Wimbledon. While they seemed to have gone off the boil we were enjoying a marvellous run, and were unbeaten since that defeat at Manchester United on New Year's Day. Boosted by the win in the Cup final we were within sight of the double.

Both sides started cautiously and when Ian Rush picked up a knock, I came on as substitute. It was 0–0 at half-time but seven minutes into the second half Arsenal went ahead through Alan Smith. We knew Arsenal needed to score again and were happy to sit back. Perhaps we didn't realise how tired we were, or how much had been taken out of us by the emotion of the last couple of months and the physical strain of playing so many games in the last few weeks. Whatever the reason, we were below our usual standards, and looked jaded where usually we were so sharp.

Had we scored it may have given us the boost we needed, but with a minute to go it seemed we'd done enough. However, just when you think everything is going your way, football has a funny way of kicking you in the teeth. As the game drifted towards injury time Arsenal made a last attack. The ball bounced favourably for Michael Thomas and he had a clear run at goal, slipping the ball past Bruce Grobbelaar to give Arsenal victory and the title. The last kick of the last game of the season had settled the championship.

We were stunned. There was barely time to kick-off again before the referee blew the final whistle. As Arsenal celebrated the Liverpool players looked shattered and trudged slowly back to the dressing room. We knew we'd thrown the title away, especially having been in the driving seat on the night. Most of the lads sat quietly staring at their boots. It was devastating, and although other events earlier in the year had taught us to put disappointments like this into perspective, it didn't ease the pain at that moment.

Perhaps our biggest mistake was in beating West Ham so convincingly on the Tuesday. That gave us the cushion of goal difference advantage, which meant we could afford to lose and still be champions. With so much at stake it allowed for negative thoughts to creep in, whereas if we had needed to win we might have approached the game in a more positive style.

In the end Arsenal were worthy champions. The margin was tight though. We both had the same number of points and an identical goal difference. But Arsenal took the title because they'd scored more goals.

Over the course of the season they'd played the best football that I could remember from any Arsenal team. I knew quite a few of the Arsenal lads from trips with England and popped into their dressing room to say: 'Well done!'

It wasn't easy to hide my disappointment but I like to think that if the positions had been reversed they would have done the same. The stakes in the First Division may be higher than at park football level, but I strongly believe it is important that players remember the spirit of the game.

I was luckier than the rest of the Liverpool players because I had something to take my mind off that disappointment almost straightaway. Sandra had gone into hospital that night to have our baby. I rushed to the maternity ward after the game and the next morning Drew Peter Beardsley was born.

No thrill can compare to the excitement of becoming a parent and Drew's birth more than compensated for the footballing misery of the night before. Sandra was worried when she realised that he shared his birthday with Paul Gascoigne and we had to reassure her that not everyone born on that day is mad – although even in his first year Drew showed signs that in time he could become just as mischievous as Gazza.

It was the proudest day I've ever known. His arrival at the end of one of the most emotional seasons football has ever known was perfect timing for the start of a new and exciting chapter in our lives.

15
SO CLOSE TO GLORY

There's something special about a World Cup year. Mexico in 1986 had given me a taste of the greatest sporting event in the world, and four years later I was proud to be involved once again in Italy. Few people gave England a chance – in the end though we were to prove all the critics wrong, reaching the semi-finals, before losing to the eventual winners, West Germany, in the heart-breaking penalty shoot-out. It was the end of yet another remarkable year in my career which seemed to get more eventful by the season.

My first priority had been to help Liverpool try to win the League. After the disappointment of being pipped at the post the previous season, the players had all gone their separate ways for the summer.

Once we started pre-season training, I can't remember anyone ever mentioning the Arsenal match again. As always with Liverpool it was the next game that was the most important. Everyone was looking forward rather than backwards.

The club had maintained continuity, with only one major signing. Glenn Hysen, the Swedish international captain and defender, joined for around £650,000 from the Italian team, Fiorentina. His arrival upset Manchester United, who thought he was going there. I don't know what happened, but I was delighted he chose Anfield ahead of Old Trafford. He already spoke good English and settled in immediately. He also surprised us in training. As an established player, some of the lads had expected him to take it easy, but he was always at the front whenever we were running and, unlike the rest of us, he never complained that training was too hard!

The transfer fee was a bargain, especially when you consider that some clubs were paying around a million pounds for defenders who were nowhere near Glenn's class. An experienced international, he'd also learned from his time in Italy, and he brought an extra dimension to our game.

As he came from the continent, so John Aldridge left, joining Real Sociedad of Spain. He was a great loss, but we all knew that he'd wanted to play abroad. He was 31 years old and feared the chance had passed him by, so when Real Sociedad offered him a good contract he decided to go.

He left in style, coming on as a substitute in the game against Crystal Palace, specifically to take a penalty at the Kop end. Needless to say he scored! We gave John a marvellous send off, winning 9–0 that night.

The scoreline makes it sound easy, but on the night Palace didn't play too badly. I was playing up front, so I had a good view of the Palace attack and thought their forwards, Ian Wright and Mark Bright, caused us all kinds of problems. They both worked hard and linked well together. Palace even hit the post when we were 2–0 up. If they'd scored then it might have been a different game. Instead, we swept the ball to the other end and scored ourselves. What might have been a close game at 2–1 became a comfortable 3–0 lead, putting a result out of their reach.

The second half became a rout and we seemed to score with ease. The crowd wanted us to go on and get ten and even the Palace supporters accepted defeat with good humour. They were to have the last laugh that season though, ruining our double hopes in a dramatic FA Cup semi-final.

Despite that huge win, our League form was never as consistent as we would have liked. We lost 4–1 at Southampton where Rodney Wallace caused us all kinds of problems, and in honesty we could have conceded five or six.

With the departure of John Aldridge, an out-and-out goal-scorer, my role changed slightly. The manager expected me to score more goals. He wanted me to push forward more often, getting into positions in the opposition penalty box, and filling in the gaps left by John's absence.

We had a few disappointing performances but there were other times when we clicked and felt unbeatable. We won 4–1 away at Manchester City and 5–2 at Chelsea, who'd led the First Division early on before stumbling to a series of heavy defeats. They tried to play a sweeper system, but Graham Roberts ended up between Ken Monkou and David Lee in the centre of their defence and we found acres of space behind their full-backs. It was one of the most comprehensive wins of the season and helped us to the top of the First Division by Christmas. No one was able to topple us over the next five months and we went on to become champions.

I was enjoying a good season. England had qualified for the World Cup finals after draws away to Sweden and Poland and my sights were set on Italy. I was on course for my target of 20 goals for the season, Liverpool were on course for the League and once again the double was within our grasp. But then came that dramatic FA Cup semi-final against Crystal Palace.

I'd scored in every round, including one in our 8–0 win over Swansea in a third round replay. We'd also beaten Norwich, Southampton and QPR and now the semi-final draw had paired us with Crystal Palace. Manchester United were drawn against the Second Division's sole survivors, Oldham. The bookies were backing a Liverpool v Manchester United final and after the first half at Villa Park we were a goal up through Ian Rush and looking a sound bet for a place at Wembley.

Palace had never really threatened our goal so the way the second half began came as a shock to everyone. From the kick-off, Steve McMahon tried to hit a ball out to our left wing but it was cut out and John Pemberton, the Palace full back, set off on an amazing run. Fast, straight and direct he took the ball deep into our half, fired over a cross and, as we failed to clear, Mark Bright seized the chance to put Palace level.

That moment changed the game. I've written earlier about the lift that a goal gives a team, and from then on Palace were rejuvenated. Even when we went 3–2 ahead they never stopped and came back again to win 4–3.

If we'd come out for the second half and played possession football for the first ten minutes we would hopefully have killed off the Palace challenge. If we'd kept them out of the game for that crucial period we would probably have gone on to win quite comfortably. Instead, Palace suddenly played with a confidence that hadn't been apparent in the first 45 minutes and deserved their victory.

Not many teams score three times in a semi-final and lose. Like any changing room, things were said in the heat of the moment immediately after the game. Football is a game of passion, and those who care deeply about the game often say things when they're frustrated, which perhaps they haven't always thought through. At Liverpool though the tension was cleared straight away. The next morning, after we'd had time to think about the game, we had a brief team meeting to talk about what had gone wrong and exchange more considered points of view. Then it was on with the job in hand. With the FA Cup run over, all attention was focused on winning the League.

I had a different worry though. An injury I'd picked up three weeks earlier was showing no sign of healing. In fact, it was getting worse. It kept me out of the team for the run up to the end of the season and threatened to rule me out of the World Cup.

It began with a kick from Steve Bruce during our 2–1 win against Manchester United at Old Trafford in mid-March. He caught me on the outside of my right knee. At the time I thought it was just another knock but gradually it got worse and worse. It didn't stop me playing but every time I jarred or landed with a jump I would feel it.

The physio examined me and we went for an x-ray but nothing showed up. I played in the games against Tottenham and Southampton but the pain was growing worse and after the semi-final against Crystal Palace it was so bad I went for a scan to see if we could find out what was wrong. It revealed a stress fracture and the doctors said the only cure was rest. I thought my season was over. By now it was mid-April, the World Cup was less than eight weeks away and I had serious doubts about being fit in time.

The doctors had said it was important to rest, but Liverpool had so many injuries at the time, I was forced to keep training. Kenny Dalglish accepted that I wasn't really in a condition to play, but he couldn't afford to let me stand idle. My injury wasn't as bad as some of the others and he needed me fit in case there was an emergency. I wasn't in the team, but I travelled with the squad to every game, often as substitute.

Those few weeks were among the most frustrating of my career. I wasn't able to play, and I wasn't able to give the knee a chance to heal. To make matters worse, there was continued speculation in the newspapers about me being transferred to Leeds. Usually with transfers the player concerned is one of the last to know, and no one from Leeds or Liverpool ever said anything to me about a move.

But the stories kept appearing, and Ray Houghton heard a rumour that a policeman had seen a sponsored car with my name painted on the side, waiting for me at Leeds. The Liverpool players kept asking me what was happening, and I'm sure people thought I'd been 'tapped' but I seemed to know even less than they did. I had no wish to leave Liverpool, and my only concern was to try to get fit.

As the weeks went by, time was running out. The England manager Bobby Robson tried to reassure me about the World Cup. He phoned each week for a progress report and said he understood Liverpool's reasons for keeping me training. His support was marvellous. He told me not to worry and that once the season was over he would make sure I had three weeks rest to cure the injury. Hopefully that would leave me fit and fresh for Italy. I knew it was something that would take time, and time wasn't on my side.

Aston Villa were still on our tails in the League and kept the title open until late in the season. A lot of people were predicting that they'd crack and their challenge would fade, but they'd said the same about Arsenal the year before, and this time we weren't going to take any chances.

The manager had signed Ronnie Rosenthal, an Israeli international forward on loan from the Belgian club Standard Liege. Ronnie made an undistinguished club debut for the reserves, but his arrival in the first team was explosive. He hit a hat-trick in his first full match away at Charlton, and finished the season with seven goals in eight appearances. It was a magnificent contribution and every time he popped up in the opposition penalty area he looked dangerous. It certainly impressed the manager. He went on to sign him permanently for around £1 million.

We eventually made sure of the title a week before the end of the season. Our victory over QPR, combined with Villa being held to a draw by Norwich, made it mathematically impossible for them to catch us. With the championship safely back at Anfield, Kenny Dalglish told me to take the rest of the week off. 'Thanks for all you've done,' he said. 'I'm sorry you had to keep training, but I hope the knee heals in time for you to have a good World Cup.'

It gave me some time, but not enough before England's warm-up games at the end of the season and their departure for Italy. I was included in a squad of 26, which would eventually be reduced by four. I knew that with Alan Smith and Steve Bull in the party there was plenty of cover should my leg still be a problem.

Bobby Robson knew my position and he understood my fears. I wasn't training and came on only as a late substitute in the game against Uruguay but the manager had told me that he knew what I could do, and as long as I was fit, I'd be in the squad for Italy. It was still a great relief when he named his final 22 and my name was on the list. But it was several weeks since I'd last played a full match and as the World Cup approached I couldn't work my way into the full England team.

John Barnes was pushed forward to play alongside Gary Lineker in the final warm-up against Tunisia. The manager wanted to see how they would work together. My view may have been clouded by the fact that I wanted to partner Gary, but I've always felt that John was at his most effective when he was operating from the wing, playing deeper where he was able to run at the defence.

The manager gave me a run out in a friendly against a local Sardinian team and after I scored a hat-trick during a 10–1 win there was a sudden clamour for me to be in the team for the opening game against the Republic of Ireland. I certainly felt as though I was getting back to my sharpest but I knew the Ireland game wasn't going to be the easiest for my return to the England team.

If Liverpool were playing them I probably would have been left out of the team, as I was against the First Division's long-ball sides like Wimbledon and Millwall. As I had feared, the match was terrible, developing little above kick and rush.

We'd taken the lead early on through Gary Lineker. Ireland had never tried to create chances, hoping instead to pressurise us into mistakes. That's how they scored their equaliser when Kevin Sheedy pounced on a ball we'd failed to clear, to hit a superb shot past Peter Shilton.

The critics said England were rubbish, and by the standards we knew we were capable of, they were right. Ireland had made it difficult for us to play, as they did for every team they met. I knew the draw, and my own disappointing performance meant I would probably be out of the team for the next game against Holland.

There was growing pressure for Steve Bull to be given a game, and although he didn't start the match he was on the bench and came on as substitute. We also knew that the manager wanted to change the formation at the back, and introduce a sweeper.

He'd explained even before the competition started that the Ireland game was a one-off and he'd picked his team specifically for that match. The Irish pushed their opponents so far back that there was no room for a sweeper behind the defence. There were strong hints that we would play a sweeper in other games and in the first training session after the Ireland match the manager went straight to work on it.

The players all approved. It gave us the confidence to attack a bit more, and the forward playing alongside Gary Lineker didn't have to worry so much about chasing opposition full-backs or defenders because we knew we always had a base of five to combat two or three forwards.

With extra movement up front we found we were able to create so many more options than before. It also allowed our defenders to push forward and bring the ball up from the back. the full-backs had more freedom and Mark Wright proved what a good player he was, superb as a sweeper, firm in the tackle and excellent going forward. He made such an impact that the German press immediately picked him for their World Cup XI.

Liverpool had a long line of ball-playing defenders who brought the ball forward: Phil Thompson, Alan Hansen, Mark Lawrenson and Gary Gillespie had all proved the advantage of having defenders who could create opportunities in attack.

The system worked well in the 0–0 draw with Holland, a game we were unlucky not to win. And it contributed towards the crucial winning goal in the game against Egypt. With an extra man at the back, Des Walker felt confident of taking the ball forward and he won a free-kick on the edge of the penalty area. Gazza floated it over, and Mark Wright scored with a glancing header.

Immediately, I was up and dancing around with Gazza. I was so excited that Bobby Robson had to drag me off the pitch. He sent me on again with six minutes to go and I was so keen to impress that I found myself booked. The tackle was enthusiastic, but never malicious. More importantly though, England had won.

By beating Egypt we finished top of our group and were through to the last 16. Winning the group was something of a bonus. It gave us five days to prepare for the second round game against Belgium, while Holland had only two days to recover from their match against Ireland before their next game against West Germany.

So rather than rush off to our next venue we were able to relax in the friendly and familiar surroundings of our hotel in Pula, near Cagliari. After three weeks there it had become a second home. The facilities were magnificent. Because of the high security surrounding the teams we weren't able to get out and about as much as we may have liked. Restricted to an hotel, it would have been easy to become bored, but there was so much to do we were able to relax and still keep active.

Many of the lads spent time around the swimming pool, and there were tennis courts, a golf course and a driving range. All the players were given a set of clubs from the manufacturers, Wilson, and I used mine most days. My football may not have got any better in Italy, but my golf certainly improved.

The most spectacular golf though came from John Barnes. He'd never played before but when Mike Kelly, the goalkeeping coach, organised a competition to see who could drive the ball the furthest, John entered. Most of the lads were reaching about 225–250 yards. John, who'd been given no more than a couple of lessons, came along and thumped the ball 325 yards to win comfortably. Steve McMahon won both the putting and a nine hole Stableford as Liverpool made a clean sweep of the golf trophies.

As we prepared for the match against Belgium, the players were feeling more confident. We hadn't played to our full potential but we felt we were improving. West Germany had looked the most impressive, with convincing wins against Yugoslavia (4–1) and the United Arab Emirates (5–1), but even they had been held to a draw by Colombia. So often in the World Cup teams can peak too early. It's important to pace yourself. We weren't happy with our performances, and we felt our best was yet to come.

We knew we would have to carry on without Bryan Robson. The captain, who'd been such an inspiration, had been forced to fly back to England for treatment to an achilles tendon injury. It was a cruel blow. Bryan had lasted for just one and a half games, hobbling off in the match against Holland. He tried everything to get fit, even flying out a faith-healer who'd worked wonders on him in the past. It showed how much he wanted to play for his country, but, as in Mexico four years earlier, his World Cup was ruined by injury.

His departure came as a surprise to us. We knew he'd been seeing the physio, Fred Street, every day, but then again several players were receiving treatment for knocks and we all believed that Bryan would be fit before long. It was only when reporters and photographers started saying it was big news that we realised it was serious.

One night there was a tremendous rush for the players to sign photos and footballs. I wondered why there was such a hurry and someone said: 'Haven't you heard? The skipper's going home tomorrow and we want them signed while he's still here.'

It was a disappointment to him obviously, and to the rest of the team. Bryan had been the outstanding English footballer for a decade and if he had been fully fit I'm convinced we could have gone on to win the World Cup.

Bryan's absence meant others had to assume greater responsibility. By now though Paul Gascoigne was emerging as a player of genuine world class. Never short of confidence, he had found the perfect stage for his incredible talent, and was improving in leaps and bounds with every game.

I'd known him since he was a 14-year-old with Newcastle, and it was obvious then that he had the ability. But there had always been a question mark over his temperament, and Gazza almost missed out on the World Cup until finally persuading Bobby Robson that he should go, with an outstanding performance in a friendly against Czechoslovakia. In the past he was often described as impetuous and immature, but he'd learned a responsibility on the pitch without sacrificing the individuality that was his great strength.

His enthusiasm for the game and for life in general is incredible. He's always messing around, tapping people on the top of their head and pulling their shirts during training, playing practical jokes or talking his own brand of nonsense.

During the game against Holland, he was apparently asking Ruud Gullit how much he earned, and when Ronald Koeman, one of the best players in the world, hit a couple of wayward passes, Gazza went straight up to him, asked him how much he'd cost, and told him he was a waste of money!

But that is typical of Gazza. He's always been cocky, even as a teenager in Newcastle's reserves. In those days the opposition would often include an experienced professional making a come-back from injury. Gazza, who hadn't even played in our first team, would go up to them and say: 'Pack it in! You're too old! You're finished!' This to players who'd achieved far more than Gazza could ever dream of at the time. It wasn't meant nastily, it was just part of his way of winding people up. If they took the bait, then he'd have the upper hand.

Gazza was great fun in the dressing room and kept us going when we took all the stick from the press after the game against Ireland. Some players might have been depressed, but Gazza was always on a high, always larking about and looking for something to make everyone laugh.

He's marvellous company and a breath of fresh air for three or four days, but when you're with him 24 hours a day for six weeks he can be exhausting. When we left Italy, Gazza's Tottenham colleague Gary Lineker was looking forward to his holiday more than most.

'It's alright for you lot,' he said. 'You've got a break. Another few weeks and I'll be with him again for the whole of next season!'

On the eve of a big match, Bobby Robson told the press that he'd tied Gazza to a chair so that everyone could have a rest, and that wasn't far from the truth! At the team hotel Gazza was in and out of everyone's room. I shared with John Barnes and at times we'd have to lock him out. He'd stand outside banging on the door and we'd be shouting: 'Go away, Gazza, just give us five minutes peace, please.'

Most sympathy was reserved for Chris Waddle who had to share his room with Gazza. He'd known him at Newcastle and spent a year with him at Tottenham so he knew what to expect. One evening Chris and I were being interviewed by Desmond Lynam for one of the BBC TV World Cup programmes. They came to us live at half-time during one of the games and as Des asked his first question, Gazza suddenly popped up from behind one of the cameras, pulling faces and acting the fool.

Of course the viewers couldn't see him, and nor could Des. All he could see was Peter Beardsley collapsing in a fit of giggles. It was impossible not to laugh, and I probably looked a total idiot. Des guessed what was happening and said: 'I take it Gazza's about!'

Chris did ever so well, and carried on like a true professional, answering all the questions with a straight face, while the cameraman desperately tried to keep me out of shot! Chris says he's known Gazza for so long, nothing shocks him any more.

There was never any malice in Gazza's jokes. In fact, he's a very generous man. I was with him signing autographs for youngsters when he spotted one lad who was timid and a lot shyer than the rest. Gazza went over and gave him a couple of pounds to buy himself a treat. Other lads tell tales of similar generosity. He wants everyone to have the same opportunity to enjoy life the way he does.

Gazza's growing maturity on the pitch was there for everyone to see in the second round game against Belgium. The match was into extra time and heading for penalties when the two youngest players in the England team masterminded a spectacular goal. First Gazza shrugged off his tiredness to go on yet another penetrating run into the Belgian half, and as he approached the penalty area he was brought down.

With time running out, there must have been a great temptation to have a shot. But Gazza listened to the shouts from the bench telling him to think and use the free-kick carefully. He floated a ball over the Belgian defence and David Platt span 180 degrees before hooking the ball in on the volley for one of the most dramatic goals of the competition.

This time it was Bobby Robson's turn to leap from his seat and dance a jig of delight. We were through to a quarter-final against Cameroon and just one game away from the semi-finals. We knew Cameroon wouldn't be easy – the African side had already beaten Argentina, Romania and Colombia and they'd captured the world's imagination. They had some marvellous players but we were very much the favourites.

I was one of the substitutes once again, but as the game went on we could see that John Barnes was struggling with a muscle strain. At half-time, with England 1–0 ahead through David Platt, it was obvious he couldn't continue. Don Howe told the four outfield substitutes, Trevor Steven, Steve McMahon, Steve Bull and me, to warm-up. There was a gym next to the changing room and as we went through our stretching exercises we started betting on which one of us would go on.

Trevor Steven was the favourite. We thought he would go on

and allow Chris Waddle to push forward alongside Gary Lineker. We decided that Steve McMahon was second favourite. He could go on to lock up the midfield and protect our lead. Bully was third favourite. We thought his strength in the air and powerful running might cause the Cameroon defence some anxious moments. My chances were considered minimal, and the others were joking that Chris Woods, the substitute goalkeeper, would get on before me.

We heard the buzzer calling the teams out for the second half and Don Howe looked round the door to the gym and just said: 'Peter, you're on!'

We hadn't played well in the first half and in truth could easily have been trailing two or three-one. But a place in the semi-finals was beckoning. Cameroon though had already shown their strengths in Italy and again they refused to be beaten. They had nothing to lose and started to throw people forward, coming back at us with some splendid football. It paid off for them and they scored two goals in a five minute spell to take the lead.

For a while England were struggling and we could quite easily have gone out of the competition. Mark Wright was bleeding heavily from a bad cut after a clash of heads with the Cameroon forward, Roger Milla, and with Trevor Steven on as substitute for Terry Butcher we were forced to reshuffle our defence.

But the team spirit was excellent and we found a second wind. With a new determination, typified by Gazza's surging runs at the Cameroon defence, we fought our way back into the game. Eventually Gazza became too much for the Cameroon defence to handle, and when his cross set up Gary Lineker, the Cameroon keeper brought him down before he had a chance to score.

It requires a special nerve to take a penalty in that situation. There were only eight minutes to go before full-time. Should you miss, your team would almost certainly be out of the World Cup and, in the eye of the nation, you'd forever be cast as the villain. Gary Lineker though was just the man for the occasion and struck what must have been one of the calmest penalties of the competition. With the scores level at 2–2 the game went into extra time.

I'd had a poor 45 minutes. I hadn't played much football over the last three months, and after being left out of the England team in earlier matches, I felt a little nervous. I was finding it difficult to adjust to the pace of the play, but as the match went to extra time I started to feel my way back in and make a more positive contribution. The longer the game went on the better I felt.

We finished the game the stronger side, and once again Gary's pace caused problems for the Cameroon defence, earning him a second penalty from which he scored the winning goal.

It was the first time England had qualified for the semi-finals since 1966, but there wasn't really time to celebrate. As with all our matches, we hadn't kicked off until 9 pm. Extra time meant we didn't finish playing until almost 11.30 pm and by the time we'd showered and changed, waited for the manager to finish his press conference and then driven for more than an hour back to our hotel it was half past one in the morning. There were no restrictions, and the manager was happy for the boys to have a few beers if they wanted, but we were all so tired and exhausted from the game we just wanted to go to bed!

We were due to meet West Germany in the semi-final. They'd beaten Czechoslovakia 1–0, but it wasn't the convincing performance we'd seen from the Germans earlier in the competition.

Bobby Robson had organised a network of 'spies' to watch the other teams in the World Cup and give us an idea of their strengths and weaknesses. Dave Sexton had watched West Germany and he reckoned the best way to combat them was to attack from the start. He gave us a talk and said that although they were a good side they would be vulnerable at the back.

We all had our ideas about the team Bobby Robson would pick. I knew we'd have a sweeper and wondered whether he'd have room for me. Ironically my room-mate John Barnes was injured, which gave me the chance.

John had been a marvellous room-mate. We were good friends and had shared for three years at Liverpool. When things aren't always going your way it's good to have a friend around. John gave me a lot of encouragement when I was out of the team and I like to think I helped him as well. At night time we used to stay awake chatting about the game, the team, who's doing well and who's struggling. Like me, John tends to keep himself to himself, and is happy to get on with the job. He took some terrible criticism in the newspapers, and I felt many of the attacks were unfair. I have so much respect for the man, and I've never seen a more skillful player. For season after season he'd proved he was the best footballer in the country.

John's injury ruled him out of the semi-final and on the morning of the game the manager ended the speculation by telling me I was in the team. He said he wanted me to link with the midfield and help Gary Lineker up front, getting into the box as often as I could, which is the role I feel happiest in. He told me he knew I could do it, but he didn't need to bolster my confidence any more. Being selected gave me all the confidence I needed. In the 75 minutes I'd played against Cameroon I had proved to myself that I was fit enough and once again I was feeling sharp in training.

It was the most important game that any of us had ever played for England, but for once the pressure was off the team. For the first time in my England career we were going into a game that we weren't expected to win. The Germans were the favourites to win the World Cup and some of our fiercest critics were saying that as long as we didn't get battered three or four-nil, we'd do well!

The players were more confident than that. Peter Shilton was convinced we could win the competition, and with big Terry Butcher revelling in his role as captain, their confidence was spreading through the team.

From the moment I walked out onto the pitch I knew we were going to play well. The atmosphere, the stadium, the mood among the players all gave it the full sense of occasion and I've never known an England team go into a match so relaxed and confident about putting on a good show.

We followed Dave Sexton's advice and attacked from the start, causing the Germans a number of problems. It was our best football of the tournament and as the game went on the belief that the game was there for the taking grew even stronger. West Germany came back at us but at half-time we felt we were the better team.

Fourteen minutes into the second half though Germany took the lead, thanks to a huge slice of luck. Brehme's shot from a free-kick took a deflection off Paul Parker, looped up into the air over Peter Shilton and dipped under the cross-bar.

Many people have said our semi-final was one of the best games of the competition and we continued to press forward convinced we could score. Ten minutes from time, Gary Lineker put us level, making space for the shot and then steering the ball into the far corner. For the next ten minutes we were the stronger side and again in extra time we had our chances. Chris Waddle struck a beautiful shot that swerved at the last minute and span out off the post.

It wasn't to be Chris Waddle's day. The game went to penalties, and although we scored from our first three, Stuart Pearce missed to leave the Germans in the driving seat. Chris took our final penalty and hit it over the bar. The Germans were through to the final, our run was over.

Both Chris and Stuart were inconsolable and probably felt that they'd cost us a place in the final. That wasn't true. We'd gone out as a team and there was no blame on any individual. We should have won the game over 90 minutes or at least during extra time. I was the second England player to take a penalty and strangely enough I felt quite relaxed. People said it was brave, but I was quite happy to go so early. Nobody remembers if you miss early on, and the shoot-out only hots up on the fourth and fifth penalties.

It would be unfair if people remembered Chris and Stuart for one mistake, when they should be remembered for the magnificent contribution they had both made throughout the World Cup.

The other semi-final was also decided on penalties, Argentina beating a superior Italian side. Once again the value of the penalty shoot out came into question. As I saw it, the view can depend on whether you win or lose. Ireland beat Romania on penalties and were quite happy with the system. It does seem unfair but I don't know that there's a better way. The suggestion that you play on until one team scores is equally unfair on the players.

It's bad enough running around for 120 minutes. By then everyone is drained. If you played on with no time limit it could become silly. Whoever wins will be so shattered they would find it difficult to recover in time for the next match.

The England players were obviously disappointed to lose in the way we did, but Bobby Robson told us to be proud of what we had achieved. I thought it had been a magnificent match, played in a great spirit, especially with so much at stake. Guido Buchwald, who was marking me, was not only a marvellous player but a true sportsman. He wished me luck before the match and applauded good English moves. I always try to play the game in that spirit but it's rare to be marked by such a quality defender with the same sporting attitudes.

I had so much respect for the player by the end of the game that

I broke my rule of never giving away my England shirt. He was the first player outside the home countries that I've ever swapped with. Normally I keep my England shirts because they mean so much to me. But in the chaos that followed the penalties, Buchwald broke off from the German celebrations to come and find me and say: 'Hard luck!' I appreciated that, and was delighted to swap with him.

Generally I had found it quite a clean World Cup. The game against Ireland was hard, but there was no elbowing or kicking. And the Cameroon players had been quite funny when they were leading 2–1. As we were going through a bad patch they kept saying: 'Come on, play football. Play soccer.' It was only when they were 3–2 behind that they started to kick lumps out of us. The number four, Benjamin Massing, was frightening and the number 14, Stephen Tataw, gave me a terrific clout with his elbow in an off-the-ball incident as I was running towards their penalty area. But on the whole I escaped without getting clattered too often.

And the spirit of the game was lifted even higher with our third and fourth place play-off with Italy in Bari. We lost 2–1 but it was an enjoyable game with some great football.

During the game the England bench joined in the Mexican wave as it went round the ground and after the game the two teams went on a lap of honour together. There was a huge party in our dressing room with the Italians desperate to find English souvenirs. They wanted to swap shirts, shorts, socks and even jock-straps. And they were almost fighting over our track-suits. We were supposed to wear ours on the flight home for publicity pictures and when Bobby Robson saw what was happening he tried to intervene, but by then it was far too late.

The final was disappointing. Argentina didn't seem to want to play, and I was delighted that West Germany won. It would have been nice if England had been there, but I came home with some marvellous memories and a medal for our fourth place.

I don't think any of the England players expected the reception we received when we landed at Luton. Our wives had come back from Italy on the same flight. They set off for our hotel on a different coach while we were taken on an open-top bus for a quick trip around Luton. The organisers said it would take about 30 minutes, but there were so many people the bus could hardly move. Tens of thousands turned out to see us, greeting us like heroes.

I was proud to be part of the England set-up. And I was pleased that we'd done so well in Italy. After eight years of criticism Bobby Robson finally received the praise he deserved before leaving to join the Dutch club PSV Eindhoven. I was thrilled for him.

And I was thrilled that the game I love was still so popular across the country. It's still the best sport in the world and I'm lucky that in the past I've been able to spend my life doing what I enjoy most. When I look back to my faltering start as a professional footballer I'm amazed that I've come so far. It really has been a dream come true.

PHOTOGRAPHIC ACKNOWLEDGEMENTS

The authors and publishers would like to thank the following for their permission to reproduce copyright photographs (identified by caption):

Action Images: A moment of relaxation in Italy; the play-off for third place

AllSport: Ray Wilkins; another late starter – Chris Waddle; England v Poland in Monterrey, World Cup, 1986

Empics: Gary Lineker's goal against the Republic of Ireland, World Cup 1990; to go out to West Germany on penalties was heartbreaking

Loftus Brown: 13 was my lucky number for three years in Canada

Colorsport: Playing for Vancouver; Keven Keegan was an inspiration; Alan Hansen has consistently been one of the best defenders in the game; 'Jinky' Jimmy Smith; Beardsley, Barnes and Aldridge; backed up by Steve Hodge and Mark Hateley; markers stick close at international level; holding off a close challenge from Ronnie Whelan; I though we were unlucky to lose to Holland

Fotosports International: My first encounter with a South American defender

Bob Thomas: Sandra shares my big day; a reminder to the opposition; Roy Evans helps me off the pitch; I score the second goal in England's 3–0 win against Paraguay; a 3–0 win against Poland revived our World Cup hopes; Bobby Robson was relaxed before the World Cup quarter-final against Argentina; in action against Argentina, June 1986; one of my proudest moments; I saw Paul Gascoigne develop from a schoolboy at Newcastle; my first goal for Liverpool; our semi-final against West Germany

INDEX

INDEX

OTHER FOOTBALL BOOKS FROM STANLEY PAUL

☐ *Against the Odds*
An Autobiography
Bobby Robson with Bob Harris   **£12.99**

This is Bobby Robson's own story: eight years of highs and lows as the England manager. An honest and forthright book from the man with the 'hardest job in football'.

☐ *The Book of Football Quotations*
Peter Ball and Phil Shaw   **£7.99**

If you want to know what Peter Beardsley thinks of John Barnes or what Bobby Robson said about Maradona, you need look no further. Here are the greatest names in football, past and present, talking about each other and the game they love.

☐ *Clough*
A Biography
Tony Francis   **£6.99**

Brian Clough is no ordinary football manager; this book tells the story of the most inspiring and quotable figure in football. 'An outstanding example of its kind, the product of exceptionally diligent research' – *Sunday Times*.

☐ *The Dons*
The History of Aberdeen Football Club
Jack Webster   **£8.99**

First published in 1978 to mark Aberdeen Football Club's 75th anniversary, Jack Webster has brought the story right up to date, showing how the Dons have established a new power base in Scottish football.

OTHER FOOTBALL BOOKS FROM STANLEY PAUL

☐ *Extra Time and It's Still a Funny Old Game*
Ian St John and Jimmy Greaves   **£4.99**

TV's most popular soccer pundits, Saint and Greavsie, take a hilarious new look behind the scenes of big-time football. Nostalgic for the great names of the past is spiced with salty comments on the game today and on such current stars as Paul Gascoigne, Vinny Jones, Bryan Robson and John Barnes.

☐ *Gazza – My Life in Pictures*
Paul Gascoigne   **£5.99**

An action-packed book in which Gazza tells in his own inimitable style the story of his life so far. Including behind-the-scenes and family photographs, this is the book no Gazza fan will want to be without.

☐ *Jackie Milburn*
In Black and White
Mike Kirkup   **£12.99**

Based on the last interview that Jackie Milburn gave four months before he died, Mike Kirkup reveals the private face of a man wanting to put the story straight once and for all. 'Wor Jackie's name will live forever when mine has faded with the passing of time' – Bryan Robson

☐ *Saint and Greavsie's World Cup Special*
Ian St John and Jimmy Greaves   **£4.99**

Saint and Greavsie's day-by-day diary of the 1990 World Cup finals is packed with authoritative comment, graphic descriptions and an hilarious and irreverent look at the off-beat moments of the tournament. Lavishly illustrated with action photographs and cartoons.